"Paul Kurts raises important ques  xposing **The Myth** that need to be aske k to the Gospel of Grace to provide the tinue to lead people away from legalism."

Dr. Joseph Tkach,
Grace Communion International,
Glendora, California.

"Paul Kurts reveals his pastoral heart in laying out a scriptural case for the love, grace and patience of God trumping popular religious concepts of divine wrath, revenge, and eternal punishment. **HELL LETTERS -Exposing The Myth** is not a theological treatise, but it is a mighty encouraging Bible-based sermon."

Dr. J. Michael Feazell,
San Jacinto, California.

"Many spiritual leaders today fail or fear to speak directly to historical facts concerning the origin of certain traditional teachings of the Christian Church. They fear even opening their eyes and ears in order to examine long held concepts which were designed primarily for the purpose of controling others rather than setting them free to know the ONE, TRUE GOD - FATHER, SON AND HOLY SPIRIT! Paul Kurts in this new work, **HELL LETTERS - Exposing The Myth,** examines the false concept of "HELL and ETERNAL TORMENT or PUNISHMENT" and their pagan origins. In this work he links the pieces of the puzzle together in such a way to illuminate the ONE, TRUE GOD--Who is LOVE, LIFE ETERNAL, and HAPPINESS for all of mankind. Truly freeing."

Dr. Stanley D. Murphy, Ed.D,
Argosy University,
Nashville, Tennessee

"**WARNING:** Do NOT read this book if you are in love with your traditional view of 'hell' - it will only infuriate you! My Dad has dedicated much of his life to exposing one of the most destructive and unbiblical teachings in the body of Christ - that God has prepared a place of fiery and eternal torture for those who do not return His love. This teaching has driven more people away from God than perhaps any other in church history. Shame on us! It is high time the church took more seriously God's salvation plan for all humanity than we do our beloved 'hell'. I highly recommend a thoughtful reading of **HELL LETTERS - Exposing The Myth** as long as you do not mind having your deeply rooted beliefs challenged."

Major Paul David Kurts,
USAF, Senior Pastor New Beginnings,
Hickory, North Carolina.

"Having served in the ministry for over forty years and being an educator for a couple of decades I have always realized the importance of simplicity in the presentation of material. As individuals we need the truth on subjects to be easily comprehended and especially those things dealing with our spiritual lives. Paul is gifted in getting to the core of subjects and condensing them into short concise statements and information that a person leaves feeling," I understand that now as never before."

How many of us have dealt with the concept of the fear of "HELL"? As a child I was always fearful that God was going to get me if I slipped up and I would be sent to a fiery place of torment if I did wrong. This causes us to take our eyes off of the loving Father God to a God we fear. I feel that Paul's new book, **Hell Letters – Exposing The Myth**, is a well presented book that to me is a handy reference that condenses and shows a person the truth about "Hell." The way he shares the information exposes the myth, but also gives the reader references to where they can research the subject for themselves. If a person, Christian or otherwise, reads this 'manual' with an open mind and asks God to let them **see** the truth regarding this very important subject through the eyes of truth they will be blessed with the joy of not having to fear God in the wrong way. The additional letters concerning Trinitarian Theological understanding are outstanding and exciting to read. This new book of Paul's and his excellent book, **TRINITARIAN LETTERS: YOUR ADOPTION AND INCLUSION IN THE LIFE OF GOD,** present one of the best presentations of who the God of love really is as Father, Son and Holy Spirit. I highly recommend these to my congregations and those truly seeking a simple yet factual understanding of Hell and the Trinity. It is with pleasure that I endorse this excellent book."

Frank S. Parsons, AA, BA, MEd. EdS,
Senior Pastor New Beginnings Christian Fellowship,
Big Sandy, Texas.

HELL LETTERS:
EXPOSING THE MYTH

How Hell Got Into The Church And The
Good News Of The Original Gospel

PAUL KURTS

WESTBOW
PRESS
A DIVISION OF THOMAS NELSON

www.hellletters.com

WestBow Press books may be ordered through booksellers or by contacting:

WestBow Press
A Division of Thomas Nelson
1663 Liberty Drive
Bloomington, IN 47403
www.westbowpress.com
1 (866) 928-1240

Because of the dynamic nature of the Internet, any web addresses or links contained in this book may have changed since publication and may no longer be valid. The views expressed in this work are solely those of the author and do not necessarily reflect the views of the publisher, and the publisher hereby disclaims any responsibility for them.

Any people depicted in stock imagery provided by Thinkstock are models, and such images are being used for illustrative purposes only. Certain stock imagery © Thinkstock.

Scripture taken from the King James Version of the Bible.

Scriptures taken from the Holy Bible, New International Version®, NIV®. Copyright © 1973, 1978, 1984, 2011 by Biblica, Inc.™ Used by permission of Zondervan. All rights reserved worldwide. www.zondervan.com The "NIV" and "New International Version" are trademarks registered in the United States Patent and Trademark Office by Biblica, Inc.™ All rights reserved.

ISBN: 978-1-4908-1446-9 (sc)
ISBN: 978-1-4908-1447-6 (e)

Library of Congress Control Number: 2013919944

Printed in the United States of America.

WestBow Press rev. date: 11/14/2013

CONTENTS

ABOUT THE AUTHOR

Paul was born, along with a twin sister, Pattie, in Philadelphia, Mississippi in 1944. The family soon moved to Jackson, Mississippi where the children grew up. Over the years Paul had many varied interests in his life. Participating in music, choir, band, symphony and many youth sports of baseball, basketball, tennis and collegiate golf. He later coached baseball, basketball and instructed golf professionally for over 40 years.

Paul graduated from Mississippi State University in 1966 with majors in Political Science (pre-law) and Psychology. He graduated from Ambassador University in 1972 with a Theology degree. Paul has an honorable discharge from the United States Air Force and still maintains an interest in flying with a private pilot's license. Other interests include writing poetry and a love of learning. Paul is a past member of the T.F. Torrance Theological Fellowship.

With his wife, Pat, the Kurts have pastored Grace Communion International churches around the eastern United States for over 40 years. Now retired from full time pastoring Paul devotes much spare time to studying and writing on Trinitarian, Adoption and Inclusion Theology—an understanding of God's Love for all of humanity and His plan to have mankind live inside of His life forever made a reality for all by Jesus Christ.

The Kurts have three grown children, Pastor Paul David, Michael Shane and Dr. Allison K. Kurts Meadows and three grandsons, James Paul Kurts, Michael David Kurts and Maxwell Wesley Meadows.

Paul continues speaking engagements around the country sharing God's Love for all people.

Paul is also the author of **Trinitarian Letters**-Your Adoption and Inclusion in the Life of God. Westbow Press, 2011. Web site at:

www.trinitarianletters.com

And, **Poems of Love, Life and Laughter,** Westbow Press, 2012.

DEDICATION

There is only ONE Truth in all of creation and that Truth is a Who not what!! I wish to dedicate this book to everyone who is mature enough and broad minded enough to put away error and falsehood and embrace the eternal truths that are found only in Jesus Christ. May God bless your continued study as you continue on into a new dimension.

Paul

INTRODUCTION

People are so passionate about what they believe, no matter the source, that they had rather 'fight than switch' as the saying goes. "I have been good all my life, not doing this, that or the other thing and by God I deserve Heaven. Now, others who have been drinking, having sex, committing adultery, fornicating, doing drugs, stealing, lying, cheating and any number of other evils, don't tell me that they are not going to hell. They have earned it and I have earned heaven."

People are PASSIONATE about their belief in hell. Somehow for them it is the eternal equalizer. "Those people deserve hell and I don't." Some get almost belligerent defending their concept of hell. They deserve heaven and others who are reprobate deserve hell. Could this all be boiled down to a degree of self-righteousness on the part of "good" Christians? Whether hell exists or not has no bearing on the reality of Satan and his present work on this earth. Satan absolutely exists as the great deceiver walking the earth as a roaring lion of destruction. The question is does an ever burning, torturing, damning hell fire exist and has it always existed? The Truth is truly freeing!

We categorize sin. Some not so bad. Some really bad. God does not. Sin is Sin. And ALL of it was forgiven at the Cross of Christ— past, present and future. When we start to categorize sin as bad and not so bad, we are right back into Greek Mythology and works and we have left the Grace train at the station.

People love their hell. I probably will not do much about that in this little book. But the truth remains. They love their hell. For whatever reasons.

But the Truth is freeing. Not only for the individual, but for all of humanity. God is love and He loves all of us the same as He loved Jesus. (See. John 17;23.). The Good News really is **GOOD NEWS** for EVRYONE.!!!

FOREWORD

When I was a child I understood and believed from a child's viewpoint. To me Santa Claus, Mickey Mouse, Man in the Moon and any number of other things were **very** real to me. Even the concept of **'hell'** was real to me and I was terrified of the thought of ever going there. As with all myths about things we believe or think we understand they are, for a time, real to us.

As Paul says in I Corinthians 13:11, "When I was a child, I understood as a child, I thought as a child: but when I became a man, I put away childish things."

The same thing can be said of all of us. As we grow in spiritual maturity we learn many things that we once thought to be true we find out in time that they were not true or accurate and that we need to change how we look at things in light of new understanding. We can call it growing in maturity in our Christian walk. A closed mind can **never** be taught new understanding since it thinks it knows all there is to know. It is a sad condition indeed. Mentally locked in the confines of one's mind believing in the same things one did as an immature child is a pitiful state to be sure.

We all know that Santa Claus, Mickey Mouse, the Man in the Moon as well as the moon being made out of blue cheese are all non-realities. They do **not** exist in truth but in our mind's eye at one time they did. Satan, on the other hand, very much exists. He is the great deceiver. He and his demons are ever active in the world. Paul calls him, "the god of this world". (II Corinthians 4:4; Ephesians 2:2;

I Peter 5:8; II Peter 2:4; Revelation 12:9). Satan is **very** active here on planet earth along with his demons influencing the evil that continues on in the world. (Ephesians Chapter 6).

So what then about the concept of an ever burning, torturing, horrific eternal punishing **hell fire** for the "lost" or "unsaved"? Can we ask ourselves, 'Would an all loving God, Who loves **unconditionally,** relegate most of His own children to such a fate? Or is it possible that in His great love for His creation and His children He had a plan that through His coming to man's rescue would be able to actually **SAVE** His fallen creation, man included, and provide an eternal existence with Himself in a heavenly relationship sharing His divine nature with mankind forever?

The early New Testament church grew rapidly for the first 500 years from its inception at Pentecost in 31 A.D. without any doctrine or concept of an ever burning tormenting hell in its theology. The love of God for all people and the forgiveness of all of their sins was enough to draw people to the Savior and for them to experience that mutual relationship with Him and each other. The **fear** of any afterlife of fire and torture was not part of the equation. This book will show **how** the idea came into the church beginning in the 5th century and **why.**

This book is really two books in one writing. One is on the non-reality of the common concept of 'hell' and the second part in on the authentic GOOD NEWS and the Adoption and Inclusion of all humanity into the life of God.

With this information please feel free, as I know you will, to make your educated decision as to the reality or non-reality of **'HELL'.**

God Bless Your Sincere Studies,

Paul Kurts
Author

P.S. Since this book is a book of "letters" there will be some redundancy in the contents of some of the letters. Maybe that emphasis is what is needed.

PREFACE

There is something greatly wrong in the Christian church today. In many areas of the Western world the church is not only not growing, it actually is going backwards and dying a slow death both physically and spiritually. Many unbelievers are turned off by the idea that a loving God would choose to burn individuals in an ever burning hell fire of torture and torment because they did not choose to acknowledge Him as the true God and invite Him into their life. They just will not have anything to do with a God like that. Most people in this post-modern world are not interested in God or religion at all. Jesus may be the light of the world, but to them darkness feels so much better! They do not want to hear about a God who, to them, appears anything but a God of love. With an ever burning 'hell' concept in the church's doctrine the Good News is anything but Good News.

In reality the church was taken captive by Augustinian theology when the doctrine of 'hell' and eternal torment were introduced into the church by St. Jerome in the late 300's A.D. with the translation of the **Latin Vulgate** and its acceptance by St. Augustine in the 400's A.D. (More on this will be covered in the remaining pages of this book.) This "hell" of a theology hijacked the church and took it on the theological journey away from the unconditional love of God and into the 'reward and punishment and heaven and hell' challenge. God and Satan would now be in competition for the souls of men with **man** determining man's eternal fate. The original plan of God to **Adopt and Include** all mankind into the life of the Father, Son and Spirit, made a reality by the life, death, resurrection and ascension of Jesus Christ would be pushed to near obscurity by this 'Greek Mythological' concept put into the church. Many New Testament Christians would be put to death as heretics for rejecting this neo-Greek Mythological Christian church and its authority over their life. These early martyrs would have no fear of death or the threats of the church as they knew their security and the assurance of their salvation and eternal home would be with God. (See Hebrews 2:15).

My personal walk out of the Augustinian Captivity with its fear tactic of 'eternal torment', ie, hell, has been the most freeing experience one could imagine. Coming into the glorious **Light** of the truth that is Jesus and understanding how much The Triune God loves not only me, but ALL of His children and understanding that the 'authentic gospel' is a gospel of love and the unconditional love of God for all of humanity, **you** included, truly sets one free. "Free at last, Free at last. Thank God Almighty we are free at last". (John 8:32).

I wish to thank a number of people who have been instrumental in helping me come to the understanding I now have. I wish to thank Dr. Joe Tkach, Pastor General of Grace Communion International, for having the courage to always stand for truth no matter what the consequences. I so much appreciate his love and friendship. Also, Dr. J. Michael Feazell who saw the truth of God's love for everyone and wrote about it some 15 years ago. I also want to recognize Dr. C. Baxter Kruger, director of Perichoresis, for his amazing books on the application of Trinitarian Theology in one's life. (The Great Dance, The Secret, The Parable of the Dancing God, Jesus and the Undoing of Adam, God is For Us, Across all Worlds, and his latest, The Shack Revisited.). Dr. Kruger has been a friend and teacher to me for going on seven years. I want to express my sincere thanks and appreciation to my loving wife, Pat, for being patient with me for my incessant discussion of the 'hell' topic.

Lastly, but not least, I want to thank the Holy Spirit for teaching that Universal Reconciliation of all things in the blood of Christ is an accomplished fact. (Colossians 1:20). Also, that Universal Salvation in **HOPE** for all of mankind is the desire of our loving Father in Heaven.

May your journey out of darkness and into Light be as wonderful for you as it has been for me.

God Bless.

Paul

LAZARUS

What about Lazarus? Doesn't that parable prove heaven and hell? Since there has been much written concerning the parable of Lazarus and the Rich Man explaining the real meaning of the parable which has nothing to do with hell and eternal torment, I will not devote lengthy discussion in this book. The bottom line of the parable is the difference in serving and being served, of giving verses getting, respect verses disrespect showing that a great gulf exists between any of these stated here.

A study of Greek words from the original translations, NOT the KJV, will show quickly that the parable is not about any kind of hell. With this being said, I shall leave this discussion to a future time. If one were to take the parables and sayings of Jesus in the KJV as authentic truth, then He spoke of "hell" as frequently as any other topic and probably more. The rest of this book will demonstrate why this is not the way to understand the truth of scripture. The Augustinian-St. Jerome 'hell' bias is all throughout the KJV stemming from the translation of the Latin Vulgate from 382 A.D. More will be said about this later in this book.

The point here is do you want the truth of the REAL Gospel, the authentic Gospel, or do you prefer to remain in whatever degree of ignorance you find yourself with your head in the sand and clinging to old falsehoods and old paradigms?

Be of good courage. Take off your blinders. Open your heart to let Jesus Christ and The Holy Spirit speak to you. Prayerfully study this eye opening book. You shall know the Truth and the Truth shall set you free. (John 8:32).

WHERE DO YOU GET YOUR TRUTH?

"I am the Way, the Truth, and the Life." Jesus proclaims in John 14:6. Most all Christians can quote this verse. But most all of us are not aware of the RADICAL nature of this statement of Jesus.

By way of comparison this would compare today to some Professor of Logic or Philosophy stating that EVERYONE else is wrong in their philosophies and logic and that ONLY he now has the true understanding of the way things are, the nature of God, the beginnings of the Universe, the final resting place and state of the dead, and essentially ALL other questions of life and the existence of the Cosmos.

In reality he would be saying he is the light of the world. He is the ONLY one in which TRUTH reposes. Radical! Yet, when we look at the life of Jesus and His claims this is exactly what He did in his earthly ministry.

A little back ground. By the time Jesus came onto the scene there had been literally hundreds of philosophers and teachers parading through history with any and every kind of doctrine, philosophy, and "truth" imaginable. Everything from why the Cosmos was made in the first place, how it was made, from what it was made, the inception of evil into the creation, the afterlife of those doing good and the afterlife of those doing evil during their lifetime.

There was no shortage of "thinkers" the world had produced in the thousands of years before Jesus. There was one philosopher, however, who in his education and mental brilliance embodied the composite teachings of the 'best' of the ancient philosophers.

3

He wrote on just about every subject imaginable. The Western world patterned its thinking after the elements of this man's teaching. He wrote numerous treaties dealing with all aspects of life. He introduced the concept of "hell" as a place of eternal infernos of punishment for evil. His works included, Protagoras, The Republic, Apology, Phaedo, Timaeus, Symposium, The Laws, and Gorgias. This was a brilliant man. Respected. Admired. Followed. Revered. Acclaimed. And mostly WRONG. The man was Plato of Athens Greece who lived 400 years before Christ.

Plato's teachings were just accepted as the way things are. They were considered the map and highway to a positive after life experience. Heaven if you will. A state of eternal bliss. Plato was considered a teacher of truth.

Jesus comes on the scene in His ministry in about 30 A.D. and with His teachings explodes the concepts of ALL philosophers before Him including Plato when Jesus says, "I am the Way, the TRUTH, and the Life. No one comes to the Father—or gets to the heavenly afterlife—but by and through ME." Talk about radical. In this one statement Jesus repudiates EVERYTHING in the entire society they had come to believe. He is not making friends to say the least. Paul later does the same thing in Athens—Plato's home town—in Acts 17.

Paul further warns us concerning philosophy which mitigates against the Truth that is in Jesus in Colossians 2:8, ""See to it that no one takes you captive through hollow and deceptive philosophy, which depends on human tradition and the basic principles of this world rather than on Christ."

Why is all this important for us today? There are only two ways anything can be understood and explained when it comes to the Bible, doctrine, or theology. The first way is what Paul calls 'the basic principles of this world' which starts from the wrong premise of human reasoning. The second way to understand these principles is to begin with the TRUTH. The Truth is in Jesus. (Ephesians 4:21). We must start with the Creator God. The Triune God. Father, Son, and Holy Spirit. With His overflowing Love. With the fact that All things were created by, through, and for Jesus Christ and that He upholds and sustains ALL Creation. (Colossians 1:16-17). That He is LOVE. That He Adopted mankind and redeemed mankind and included mankind in His life before the foundation of the world. Before creation of the cosmos. (Ephesians 1:3-14). Take your choice. Take God or man. Who's your daddy?

Philosophy of the world is complex and convoluted. The TRUTH that is in Jesus is simple. It is not rocket science. Paul says it this way in II Corinthians 11:3, "But I fear, lest by any means, as the serpent beguiled Eve through his subtlety, so your minds should be corrupted from the **simplicity** that is in Christ."(KJV).

This is all important to us because modern Christianity has taken many of its concepts from the pagan world, especially from Plato. The truth is not in Plato. It is in Jesus.

The world has been redeemed and reconciled in Christ. Salvation for all mankind is a reality not a possibility. The Kingdom was prepared from the foundation of the world for **ALL** to enter. The question is: "Will you believe and choose to enter?"

IS THIS YOUR VIEW OF HELL—REALLY?

The view of God and the reward of the wicked by **SOME** people goes like this:

"I am God and everyone had better accept the sacrifice of my Son Jesus Christ and live in obedience to my Laws from then on or I can't begin to tell you how horrible it is going to be for you for all eternity." And by the way, for any of you who do not hear about my LOVE and my Son, you are going to Hell and suffer.

If you don't make it to heaven, then a Hell you cannot imagine awaits all of you heathen ungodly reprobates. And it is going to be gruesome. Flames much hotter than the sun in its full brightness and heat. Scorching flesh day and night with no relief ever in all of eternity. No rest. Just extreme torture and punishment for you who are wicked.

My Son only died and rose again for those who are going to heaven. He did NOT die and pay any sacrifice and payment for the rest of you who are so ungodly and sinful that evil is all you can think of and do. So you are going to burn. I am a just God and I say you must be punished for all of your evil deeds FOREVER. In your seventy or so years on the earth you earned the horrors of Hell and Hell's fury and wrath FOREVER because you were thoroughly bad and evil. I have reserved a place for all of you who are ungodly at the table of justice and you will eat of perishing fruit day and night with no respite or relief as you agonize and suffer eternally out of my sight FOREVER. I don't want to have anything to do with you. You are

7

like illegitimate sons and daughters to me. I can't stand the thought of you. I just want justice for all of you incorrigibles in torturous flames FOREVER.

I remind you, however, that I am LOVE. Love is my chief characteristic and I am fair. But because you will not love me back and you have rejected my dear son then you will not see my love, only my WRATH, but I will administer it in LOVE. Weep and gnash your teeth. Suffer. No punishment or eternal suffering is good enough for any of you since you rejected my son and you would not invite Him or Me into your life. I cannot stand rejection and I have prepared a place for all of you who have not accepted my LOVE. That place is Hell. Burning, scorching, agonizing, suffering Hell fire FOREVER. Now who do you want to love and serve, Me the loving creator God and My son Jesus, or do you want to serve yourself and the Devil---FOREVER?"

Sincerely,
Your LOVING HEAVENLY FATHER.

Does this kind of thinking resonate with you? Does it picture a realistic view of God and His Love? Do you identify personally with this type of rhetoric?

Satan would like nothing more than for man to see God in this light. And as long as we maintain a view of 'traditional hell' these concepts of God and His love will remain.

HELL'S ORIGIN IN PAGANISM

From the ancient Chinese "Diyu", or hell, ruled by Yanluo Wang with its 18 levels of torture for the wicked to virtually most every civilization and religion since we see the idea of torment for the payment of evil deeds consistent in religious teachings.

The Egyptians had as the god of their underworld Shezmu who would inflict horrible torture to those unfortunate to be assigned to this under-world fate. As in most of the world's philosophies concerning "hell" there were many levels of torment in the Egyptians "circle of Upper Hell" as "Books of the Netherworld" about ancient Egypt show. (Check out 'Infernal Names' in history on the Web.)

The ancient Greeks' teaching on the underworld or the netherworld was refined by Plato (429-347 B.C.E). Plato divided the underworld into nine levels of torment and gave the name "Hell" to this underworld in his famous writing Gorgias. He further named Hades, the brother of Zeus and Poseidon, as its god. For one to enter this 'hell' upon death the person would have to pass through the river Acheron to begin the descent into torment in one of hell's nine levels. Plato is also credited with the creation of the concept of 'purgatory'. Some 1700 years later Dante, in his Divine Comedy (1308), would plagiarize Plato naming the entrance to his nine levels of 'hell' the river Acheron. Dante's lowest level of his hell would be the place where Satan is locked in a block of ice!

Without going into every one of history's civilizations religious practices suffice it to say that all, with very few exceptions, had the concept of one being rewarded for their good deeds outweighing their evil deeds and tormented in the underworld if their evil deeds outweighed their good. This idea of reward and punishment is just natural to the mind of fallen man.

What seems to be consistent with all of these religions is the horrible description of the types of 'demonic' torment inflicted upon those lost such as eyes being torn out, tongues being ripped out, some being boiled in oil, dismembered, dancing on fiery coals and flames, having continual thirst with no water available and the list could go on and on. This is hardly the type of thing a loving Heavenly Father would either invent or allow to occur to one of His children.

Lastly, we see that this concept of 'hell' existed thousands of years before the writing of the Holy Scriptures, before Ancient Israel or Jesus Christ. Therefore we see that the hell concept obviously came out of the fallen mind and fallen nature of mankind in PAGANISM.

Does it make any sense at all that our loving God would use pagan concepts influenced by Satan the Adversary to be an integral part of the Good News of Salvation in Jesus Christ? Or is the Good News really about Adoption and Inclusion into the life of the Father, Son and Holy Spirit of ALL of God's children all made a reality in the life, death, resurrection and ascension of Jesus Christ.? Eph.1:3–5; Hebrews 10:10.

God simply loves **YOU.** And He has since before creation. You are special to God. This is true whether or not you believe it. It is so. And it is **GOOD NEWS!!!**

HOW DID "HELL" GET INTO THE CHURCH?

When understood in the original wording of the Old and New Testaments we find that the concept of any kind of hell or eternal torment was never a part of those writings. So why is the KJV and most other translations of the Bible filled with the concept of hell and eternal torment?

In truth, Jesus never spoke of any type of punishing afterlife at all. Jesus left no one out of His salvation equation. The early New Testament leaders for nearly 500 years never taught an "eternal torment" for anyone. Clement of Alexandria (c 150 -215), Origin of Alexandria (c 185 – 254), and the great Athanasius (c. 298 – 373), and other early church leaders believed in the ultimate and complete salvation of all men.

It wasn't until the time of St. Augustine of Hippo (c. 354 - 430) and St. Jerome (c. 347 – 420) that the concept they borrowed from Plato (429 – 347B.C.E.) was put into Catholic doctrine when Jerome by order of Pope Damasus, translated the **Latin Vulgate** from earlier Latin and Greek scriptures from 382 to 405 A.D. The Church would now change from common Greek being spoken in services to LATIN. Parishioners would now be forbidden to READ Bibles, even under the penalty of punishment or execution! Everywhere in O.T. scripture where the words sheol, Hebrew for grave or unseen or hidden, were written and in the Greek Septuagint New Testament where hades, gehenna or tartaroo were written Jerome translated these words as "hell". Further, scripture such as Matt.25:46 were

11

translated as "eternal torment" when the Greek simply meant age lasting chastisement from the Greek, aonian kolasin. The same wording used to prune fruit trees to make them bear fruit. Why was this done in the first place?

St. Augustine and St. Jerome were lovers of Plato's Greek Mythology and his teachings on purgatory and hell. They saw that in previous cultures that a teaching of FEAR of being tormented forever helped keep people morally in line. They felt that it would work in the church if introduced as doctrine and that a new translation would be what would educate followers as to its veracity. In 550 Emperor Justinian declared this concept as the official position of the Roman Empire. The Latin Vulgate then became the official scripture of the church and remained until the Douay Reams translation in 1582 became the official scripture of the church. And it was even translated mostly from the Latin Vulgate. When the King James Version of the Bible was translated in 1611 mostly from the Latin Vulgate the wording remained supporting the teaching of 'hell' and eternal torment.

Words in the KJV which meant grave, pit, place of restraint, burning garbage dump were translated "hell". Those four words were, sheol, hades, tartaroo and gehenna as stated above.

A politician from Florence, Italy, Dante Alighieri wrote a poem between 1308 and 1321 entitled, The Divine Comedy. Being a Catholic and indoctrinated in the 'hell' concept stemming from Plato, he writes a horrible depiction of his idea of hell from his demented mind. Dante's Inferno in the poem is a direct plagiarism of Plato's hell from 1700 years before! Along with a wrong interpretation of Lazarus and the Rich Man, Dante's Inferno became the official position of the Catholic church on the "reality" and existence of a damning Hell Fire of eternal torment.

Some three hundred years later the Protestant Reformation occurred through the mid 1600's and the concept of Hell and eternal torment stayed in the protesting churches where it remains in most all today. It creates a fear religion and holds people in the fear of death as Hebrews 2:15 says. Furthermore, it makes God look like a monster and identifies Him with the "omni" god of Greek Mythology.

WHERE THE HELL DID
THAT COME FROM?

(Notice some redundancy here in this letter compared to the previous one. These were written years apart, but I wanted to include both to emphasize the point.)

One of the big questions which comes up in discussing Adoption, Inclusion and Salvation Theology where all mankind is included in the original plan of God before the foundation of the world is the concept of "Hell" and what happens to wicked people. Are they not going to burn forever in Hell fire? Are they going to be annihilated? While we are not going to try and discuss all aspects of the Hell question, we would like to address certain facts about the concept of an ever burning and torturing Hell.

The concept of a punishing, torturing, burning, eternal place of torment is common to most all world religions **and** civilizations stemming back to before the first recognized religion of the world called Zoroastrianism after Zoroaster from about 1700 B.C., and before for thousands of year. Going back to the time of the ancient Druids of Celtic origin in the British Isles, which predates the pyramids of Egypt, we see the concept of a torturing afterlife extant. The punishment after death would be for those whose bad deeds outweighed their good ones, a concept Satan has infected all societies with since the Garden of Eden.

The Pagan Plato, a student of Socrates, introduced the concept of a tormenting Hell fire in his writings in 400 B.C. in the famous work Gorgias. Then in the fifth century A.D. (See the Catholic

Encyclopedia article on HELL and LIMBO) Augustine, after the translation of the **LatinVulgate,** refined the idea in the Christian Church where it took root and became a common teaching. Then between 1308 A.D. and 1321 A.D. Dante Alighieri wrote the poem, The Divine Comedy, in which he described his imaginings of a torturous, burning hell punishing wicked people. His three part poem consisted of Hell and Purgatory (which he plagiarized from Plato) and Paradise. Hence, the imaginings of this type of hell are from the minds of pagan men and perpetuated through the centuries by others who wanted to keep Christians "in line" with this fear tactic doctrinally.

For the first five hundred years of the Christian church, the theology of God's love which was demonstrated in His adoption and inclusion of all mankind into his Triune Life and the salvation of all mankind through the atoning and redemptive work of Jesus Christ was the message of most all of the early church leaders. Some few, steeped in Greek Mythology, held on the the pagan concept of eternal torment stemming from their involvement in the Hellenistic world. The faithful teachers to Christ's Gospel of Adoption and Inclusion of all continued to share that Good News.

The concept of a torturing hell was not disputed during the Protestant Reformation in the 1600's since the primary protest of the reformers, Martin Luther and others, was the sale of indulgences by the Catholic Church. (An indulgence was money paid to a priest to pray someone out of purgatory and into heaven!)

Western Christianity has just bought into the torturous ever burning hell of punishment for the wicked out of ignorance of where the idea come from in the first place and from a wrong translation of the Holy Scriptures—namely the **Latin Vulgate.**

Gehenna Fire is one of the common names for hell fire. The name comes from Hinnom or the Valley of Hinnom which is located Southwest of Jerusalem. The area was historically used for the tossing of dead bodies of animals, garbage, and even people who died who were not members of any particular family and who had no one who cared anything about them for any kind of "proper" burial. This place represented a very bad ending of any human who was dumped—cast—there because it showed that they were not connected to any family who cared for them or loved them. Jesus uses this comparison of one being thrown into this Gehenna Valley, ie, valley of Hinnom, to show that not being inside of the "Party of Heaven" was a terrible end. Fires were continually burning up the carcasses and other debris that was thrown into the valley of Hinnom. People in Jesus' day would have understood better than we what He was trying to say using this analogy. Jesus was not trying to establish a doctrine of an ever burning torturous fire to forever punish the lost.

Lastly, in the Book of Revelation, we read that death and hell both are to be cast into the lake of fire. There death and the 'grave' are done away with.

My purpose here in this paper is not to try and establish a doctrinal position on the doctrine of hell, but to show some perspectives on the subject which many of us have not considered before.

We can say with assurance that God is Love and that all things can and will be made right in Jesus Christ and that all things have been reconciled in Jesus Christ and that God will conclude His plan for creation in His way and in His will based on His unending LOVE.

GREEK AND HEBREW
WORDS FOR HELL

With St. Jerome translating the Latin Vulgate, by order of Pope Damasus, in 382 A.D. from the Old Latin scriptures and the Greek Septuagint he virtually translated in every case the word 'hell' from the Hebrew and Greek words **none** of which meant hell. In the Old Testament 'Sheol' simply meant the grave or place of the dead or 'the unknown'.

The Hebrew word 'shaul' meaning 'unseen or unknown' was translated by Jerome as 'hell' as were the Greek 'hades', 'gehenna' and 'tartaroo' in the NT.

We need to understand the mind of St. Jerome and St. Augustine in the late 300's A.D. and early 400's, both had been greatly influenced by the writings and philosophy of Plato who wrote some 700 years earlier. They saw that Plato's 'hell', which he named after a Greek goddess, 'hel', and naming Hades, the brother of Zeus and Poseidon, as the god of this underworld, tended to keep people morally in line out of fear of death (Hebrews 2:15) and that this same concept would 'work' in the church. However, a new paradigm of understanding would have to be introduced into scripture since this idea of 'hell' and eternal torment was **not** in any of the earlier translations of the Bible. St. Jerome would now begin translating what would become the **Latin Vulgate** Bible. Any place he could translate words into hell, from sheol in the Old Testament to gehenna, hades, or tartaroo in the New Testament he did.

Further in Matthew 25:46 he translated "age lasting chastisement" into "everlasting punishment" from the Greek, aonian kolasin. The meaning of which is "an age of pruning, like a fruit tree to make it bear fruit, or we could say a time of transformation." Even in Revelation 22:17, we see this transforming process still going on for those "outside" the gates of the Holy City even after death. This translation would become the official scriptures in the church. It was even endorsed by Emperor Justinian in 550 A.D. as the official position of the Roman Empire. With the new translation of the Douay-Reims in 1582 and the King James Version translated 29 years later in 1611, the concept would stay since the Latin Vulgate would be a main source for these translations. A fresh understanding is now available to all who will examine the subject from an educated standpoint.

SOME OLD TESTAMENT EXAMPLES FOLLOW HERE:

Deut. 32:22	fire shall burn unto the lowest (hell). Heb. 'shaul' 'unseen nether'
II Sam. 22:6	the sorrows of (hell) compassed me about. 'shaul' or 'unknown'
Job 26:6	(hell) is naked before Him. 'shaul' 'unknown'
Pslm. 16:10	you shall not leave my soul in (hell). 'sheol' 'grave'
Ps. 55:15	"Let them, the wicked, go down into (hell). 'shaul'. 'unseen'
Pv. 9:18	Her, the prostitute, guests are in the depths of (hell). 'unseen'
Pv. 23:14	you shall deliver his, childs, soul from (hell). 'm-shaul' 'unseen'
Isa. 14:15	Lucifer shall be brought down to (hell). 'shaul' 'unseen'

SOME NEW TESTAMENT EXMPLES FOLLOW HERE:

Matt. 5:22	shall be in danger of hell fire. Gk. 'the gehenna puros.'
Matt. 5:29-30.	Body cast into hell. Gk. Gehenna. "garbage pit fire"
Matt. 23:14	...shall receive the greater damnation. Gk. 'krima', judgement
Matt. 23:15	'two fold more the child of hell. Gk. Gehnna 'worthless wretch.'
Matt. 23:33	how escape the damnation of hell? Gk. Kriseos Gehenna. Judging
Matt. 10:28	able to destroy body and soul in hell. Gk. Gehnna. Garbage dump
Matt. 25:46	go into everlasting punishment. Gk. Eonian Kolasin. 'age chastening' From kolasis (Gk.) meaning like the pruning of trees to make them bear fruit.
Mk.3:29	'in danger of eternal damnation.' Gk. 'eonian *kriseos' 'age of judging'
Mk.9:43-45	fire never quenched. Gk. Asbeston, 'unextinguished.'
Luke 16:23	In hell (Gk. hadE-the unseen). Torments, Gk. Basanois, 'ordeal'
Luke 16:24-25	...tormented in this flame. Gk. Odunasai, pained for tormented, Gk. Basanou, meaning ordeal for flame.
John 5:29	...unto the resurrection of damnation. Gk. Kriseos, judging/ decision
Acts 2:31	His soul was not left in hell. Gk. Hadou, the unseen or unperceived.
Gal.1:8-9...	Let him be eternally condemned. Gk. Anathema. A person detested.
James 3:6	(tongue) is set on fire of hell. Gk. Gehenna. Set aflame by the gehenna

II Pt.2:4	But cast the angels that sinned down to hell. Gk. Tartaroo. Place of restraint. The earth. (See I Pt.5:8 and Ephesians 6)
Rev.1:18; 6:8; 20:13; 20:14	Hell in these verses is from Gk. Hadou and Hades, Meaning the un-perceived or unseen.
John 8:32,	"You shall know the Truth and the Truth shall set you **FREE.**"

GOD'S WRATH ON THE DISOBEDIENT???

Let's talk a little here about the verse in Eph.5:6-7, "Let no man deceive you with empty words, for because of such things God's wrath comes on those who are disobedient, therefore do not be partners with them."

To understand this verse better, we need to look at a few things that Paul is dealing with here in Ephesus.

Ephesus had been a city dating back some 1400 years when Paul writes this letter. The city had been established by a migrating group of women called the Amazons who had some pretty weird and pagan practices. The Temple to the Goddess Artemis, or Diana of the Ephesians, had stood as one of the wonders of that ancient world for around 1000 years. Some of the common practices of the worship of Diana and beliefs included serving Diana and connecting spiritually with her by having sexual relations with one of the temple prostitutes—and often I might add-- believing that women were superior to men, that the wife was the head of the family and her husband. Some who either came into the new Christian church there in Ephesus or who were defending the pagan practices of the Diana worship were trying to persuade the new converts to continue in their practices associated with Diana worship. And that it was not only OK, but desired to continue to go to the temple prostitutes and practice other immoral, foolish, and vain observances.

From prison in Rome, Paul addresses these things that the new converts should NOT be involved with and warns the church

NOT to allow these persons to deceive the new converts with their idolatrous teachings and beliefs. He is showing the difference in the "kingdom of Diana" as opposed to the "Kingdom of Christ", vs.5. When Paul says in vs. 6, that God's anger or displeasure in other translations, (wrath in the NIV), would come on those who are disobedient—on those teaching these immoral practices to the new church members, he is referring primarily to those doing the false teaching. He says, "do not be partners with them" in vs.7. It may also be said that anyone who sets their heart and desire on practicing an immoral, sinful, and disobedient lifestyle would not be able to see who they are in Jesus and therefore not see or experience the Kingdom of God under those conditions.

It should be obvious to all of us that Paul is not talking to individuals in the church who sin, or are disobedient at times, since these sins are cleansed by the blood of Christ. He had addressed the question of "dead in sin" in chapter 2. And he had already described salvation by Grace and not our works in ch.2 as well. So it should be understood that Paul is not here in ch.5:6 'undoing' the grace he has already described earlier! In vs.11-13, Paul is telling the church there in Ephesus not to have anything to do with the deeds associated with the temple worship and customs and practices involved with Diana. But to expose them for what they were! And that it is/was shameful to even mention what the disobedient were doing in secret there! And, that the light of Christ would make things clear as to what the church should be practicing.

Those who take Eph.5:6 out of context and say that God's wrath is somehow going to be brought down on sinners, or the disobedient miss the point of what Paul is saying here in Ephesians.

Lastly, much of what was happening in Ephesus was generated by the spirit world which he concludes his epistle (chapter 6) with encouragement to take the whole armor of God and to stand strong in the Lord and in His MIGHTY POWER. That encouragement is still valid today.

HEBREWS 6:4-6—FALLING AWAY FOREVER?

Hebrews 6:4-6, presents somewhat of a challenge to the Trinitarian Theologians who claim redemption for all and Adoption and Inclusion for all in Jesus Christ.

Again, whenever we endeavor to explain scripture we should always approach the scripture from the standpoint of "WHO IS JESUS". What has He done TO all of creation and Why? Isolated scriptures such as these two verses in Hebrews 6 then offer a different understanding than what at first seems to be the only way they may be understood.

One of the ways Heb.6:4-6 is understood is that Jews who professed to be believers progressed to the point of full belief and acceptance of Jesus but at the last moment backed down in denial and therefore fell away from the truth and the abundant life they could have experienced in Jesus.

Another way of looking at these verses is in the "hypothetical" sense. This says that if one **could** fall away from their salvation, or deny their salvation in Jesus, or nullify their salvation in Jesus, then it would be impossible to reposition them in the state of salvation since Jesus would have to be crucified again. This would make the individual more powerful than Jesus who has redeemed the entire world and reconciled it in Himself **at the Cross! (Colossians 1:20).** So, this hypothetical approach is only that, hypothetical. Remember this is Jesus' doing, not ours. So we cannot undo what Jesus came to do and did. (Luke 19:10).

23

One way of looking at this is what did Jesus do and did He have the authority and the Power to do it and was He successful in doing what He came to do? If these presuppositions are true and correct, then it is infinitely presumptuous on anyone's part to assume that we humans can UNDO what Jesus did.

Greek philosophy, of which I have written extensively in the past, has had such a bearing on our understanding of scripture that it sometimes is difficult to dissociate that thinking from the Absolute Truth that is in Jesus. Our brains are SEARED with false premises and paradigms.

Paul is simply saying here in Heb. 6 that **IF** it were **possible** for one to fall away then this is what the picture would look like for them. But, since it is **impossible** for one to fall away from Jesus (we are in His hands, we do not have Him in our hands), Jesus is the **Guarantee** of the better covenant which is a Declaration, a Gift, based on God's Unconditional love of His creation. (Hebrews 7:22). Jesus is the **YES** to all of God's promises. (II Corinthians 1:18-22).

We have been so influenced by Plato, Platinus, Aristotle, Socrates, Augustine, and Jonathan Edwards, it is difficult for us to see the real Love of God for all of His creation and the purpose He has for all of us-----if only we will **BELIEVE.**

We need to always ask the question, Whose idea is this anyway? Whose plan is this anyway? How did He plan it out originally anyway? (II Peter 1:3-4). Can we undo His sovereign plan by our puny human efforts—either good or bad?

Final disclaimer: Some of us are of the mindset that what we have learned in the past is somehow superior to the Truth that is in Jesus... That it **WAS** the Truth that was in and is in Jesus. If that is so, then there is obviously NO room for future or further growth in the Spirit of God. We shut ourselves off. Completely. Why would we want to stand in the gap and defend **ELLEN G. WHITE? OR, JOSEPH SMITH, OR JIM JONES, OR ELMER FUDD, OR MICKEY MOUSE, OR PLATO, OR AUGUSTINE?**

The truth is only to be found in Jesus Christ. Can we just look to the Love of God and purpose He created all of humanity for in the first place for our truth? Jesus made it so. Jesus made it happen. You are Adopted, and Included in the life of God forever. Why argue with this?

Now I know some of us reading this will still argue for the principles we "**PROVED**" 40 years ago in "college". We are stuck in the paradigms of the 50's and 60's. Well, stuck is stuck. What can I say? What can anyone say? Some will go to their grave defending lies and heretics and wrong ideologies for their personal defense. For these people to admit their error is somehow demeaning or belittling to their self-worth. How foolish. Let's let the Spirit of Truth teach us and follow His lead!

MALACHI 4:3 AND
TREADING THE WICKED

Coming from old Calvinistic views of the fate of the wicked, or unsaved, Malachi 4:3 could be interpreted by some and has been by some that the 'Righteous would 'tread' upon the wicked or stomp the life out of them until they were in a state of ruin or 'ashes' under 'your' feet. Somehow verse 3 is seen as some kind of Godly approval of the righteous taking the vengeance of God out on sinful humans. Maybe we need to look at this from a different angle.

We might note here that the Hebrew word used for "tread" does not mean destruction to ruin, or punishment, or stomping the 'hell' out of someone to render them to ashes. It is the same word used for crushing grapes to make wine. It is a type of destruction to transformation.

We tread upon the wicked, all of humanity who are non-believers, whenever we share the Good News that they are Adopted, saved, redeemed, and included in Trinitarian salvation. For the wicked this Good News destroys their belief in THE LIE, but that destroying leads to the beautiful truth of all our inclusion and adoption IN Jesus. Furthermore, speaking of ashes here could be speaking of the wicked's repentance, or change of mind (metanoia, Gk) as it is referenced in other places in the Old Testament. I am not saying that this is the only interpretation of this verse. However, it would seem consistent with Jesus' Salvation for all of humanity.

Note again Malachi 4 could be describing the 'zealous' evangelizing efforts of believers who know His name—Who they are IN Jesus—and that the message is for Healing—spiritual healing—with individuals carrying the Gospel message out with the enthusiasm of a 'young calf leaping when let out of its stall!' (vs 2). Then God closes verse 3 with the statement that "I do these things!" Of course it is by God's spirit and power that the Gospel message is shared with anyone and He grants the repentance (mind change) which is coming to believe that message.

So once again in this short chapter in the last book of the Old Testament God is continuing to pour out His love on all humanity as He shares the Good News with everyone eventually.

MATTHEW 25:46 AND MARK 3:29

Two of the main verses in scripture to uphold the teaching of eternal or everlasting punishment are found in Matthew 15:46 and Mark 3:29. If taken strictly from the KJV of the Bible these do say this. However, the translation of these verses is grossly misstated in the KJV.

In the original translations of the Greek Septuagint no words are used for eternal or everlasting or punishment. When St. Jerome translated the Latin Vulgate in 382 to 405, he translated the wording as to introduce the concept of 'hell' and everlasting punishment into these verses.

The original Greek in Mat.25:46, used the Greek word, 'eonian' for everlasting and the Greek word 'kolasin' for punishment–which means chastisement. The literal meaning of these are as follows. Eonian is used for a definite period of time with a beginning and an ending— ie, age. Kolasin is from the Greek word, kolasis, which has the meaning of pruning as in the pruning of fruit trees to get them produce fruit or more fruit. A more literal translation of Mt.25:46, then would be, "…and these shall go into age lasting chastisement". Done so from a transformational, life changing or growing experience. Chastisement is not punishment. Punishment is retributive. Chastisement is to produce growth and maturity. Matthew 25:46, simply does not carry the meaning of any kind of everlasting punishment when properly understood from its original intent.

Mark 3:29, is another example of poor scholarship in translation. The KMV says, "…in danger of eternal damnation." The Greek word here for eternal is again, 'eonian', meaning 'age', or period of time. The Greek word here for damnation is 'kriseos' meaning 'judging', as in judging a matter as to make a wise decision. We get our word, 'crisis' from kriseos. So, literally Mark 3:29, is saying, "… is danger of an **age** of **judging** or coming to a decision."

Blaspheming the Holy Spirit is simply one's refusing to accept and believe what Jesus has done to, for, in and through that person. In other words, refusing to repent or change one's mind. Repent in the Greek is 'metanoia' or a mind change. To change one's mind is the real meaning. As long as someone refuses to change his or her mind as to WHO they are in Jesus, they cannot experience the joy of salvation which Jesus has provided for them. Theoretically one can remain in that position of denial forever.

CONDEMNATION--"HELL" OR UNBELIEF?

What is **CONDEMNATON?** Does scripture give the definition of condemnation? This question relates to one of the scriptures which seems to mitigate against the Truth of Trinitarian Theology of salvation, adoption and inclusion of **ALL** humanity. John says, "that some will face the resurrection of condemnation" in John 5:28. "That does it, they are going to Hell. There's your proof!" But is it?

John 5:19-45 is about the **honor of the Father** and the **validation of the Son- Jesus.**

Jesus here is showing where life comes from. Where eternal life comes from. And **how** it comes through the Son. The two dynamics discussed are **Abundant Life** (John 10:10) and **Condemnation.**

John 5:24-25, "I tell you the truth, the one who hears my word and **BELIEVES** the one who sent me has eternal life and will **not be condemned,** but has crossed over from **death** to life. I tell you the truth, a time is coming--and is **NOW** here—when the dead will hear the voice of the Son of God, and those who hear will **live.**" Here we see that hearing and **BELIEVING** Jesus moves a person from DEATH to life. This is true for a person who hears this and believes it **NOW** as well as a person who hears it and believes it "in the time that is coming." What this is saying is that EVERYONE is DEAD until each hears **THE WORD** and believes it. It is all about hearing and believing Jesus and Who we are in Jesus! So what is condemnation? Maybe we can find a Bible definition! J Let's go to John Chapter 3.

John 3 is talking about salvation and eternal life where Jesus says in verse 18 referring to Jesus the Son, "Whoever **BELIEVES** in Him is **NOT CONDEMNED,** but whoever does not believe **STANDS CONDEMNED ALREADY** because he has not believed in the name of God's one and only Son." Condemnation is simply remaining in one's current state of DEATH by continuing to exist in a state of perishing and alienation through **UNBELIEF.** This happens in this life and can also happen in life after earthly physical death and scripture here calls that rising to the resurrection of condemnation—continuing on for however long in that state of unbelief. We could just as easily call it the Resurrection of Unbelief or the Resurrection of Unbelievers. Scripture calls it the Resurrection of Condemnation". Now back to John Chapter 5.

John 5:28-29, "Do not be amazed at this, because the hour is coming when all who are in the graves will hear His voice and will come out—those who have done good (ie, heard and believed) will rise to live, and those who have done evil (ie, did Not believe) will rise to remain in condemnation **AS LONG AS THEY REFUSE TO BELIEVE!!!** In so doing they will remain in that state of condemnation in resurrection **UNTIL** such time as they come to believe—if they hopefully EVER do. (See Revelation 22:15-17).

The Triune God is not after retribution. He wants all to **Believe.** He wants all to be with Him forever in joyful abundant life. Anything short of that is **CONDEMNATION!**

THE HELL CONTROVERSY

This may be too shocking for many Christians to read. Our personal paradigms are often so set in stone that mentally and emotionally we are paralyzed to even begin to think about changing or adding to them. If this is you STOP reading NOW.

This short paper will introduce you to a truth which you may want to study more on for yourself as everything cannot be covered here. God's Love is so INFINITE that it covers ALL human beings with the promise of a Glorified existence with Him forever in the Heavenly Realm. (Ephesians 1:3-6). Jesus Christ's life, death, resurrection and ascension made this a reality for YOU and everyone else. Now to the main purpose of this paper. IF this true, and it is, HOW can the teaching of Eternal Torment, ie, "Hell" be true? This is a "hot" topic to be sure!

FACTS TO CONSIDER:

1. The word "hell" is NOT in any original translations.
2. Hell was put into the Latin Vulgate by St. Jerome in 382-405 A.D.
3. In the originals Jesus NEVER taught anything about 'hell'.
4. Hell is not mentioned as a concept in the Old Testament.
5. Hell was not taught in the first 500 years of the Christian Church.
6. The concept originated in paganism and taught by Plato (400's B.C.).
7. With St. Jerome, Pope Damasus and St. Augustine it was introduced into the Church in the 5th Century.

8. Emperor Justinian made it the official teaching of the Roman Empire in 550 A.D.

9. In c.1306–1321, Dante's poem, The Divine Comedy, mainly plagiarized from Plato's Hell, became the main teaching of the Church over the 'hell' concept.

10. In 1611, the King James Version was translated mainly from the Latin Vulgate and the Douay Rheims perpetuating the concept of hell and eternal torment.

11. With the Protestant Reformation in the min 1600's, the concept would stay.

Check out the following web sites, and many more, for more information:
www.raising hellbook.com
www.tentmaker. org
www.gci.org
www.trinitarianletters.com

THE "WAGES OF SIN" AND THE "GIFT OF GOD"

Romans 6:23 is cited by most as demonstrating the fact of a person's individual sins resulting in death and then offering the gift of God to the individual for eternal life. It is reasoned that the individual is in sins and sinful and with the proper repentance then the gift of God or eternal life is then given through Jesus Christ.

But, is this what this verse is really saying. First off, it does not say the wages of a "person's sins" are death; it says the wages of SIN, all sin, is death. That death is death for ALL humans due to the sin of the first Adam. (I Cor. 15:22). The condition of death is the state all humans have found themselves in since the first Adam. The next part of the verse 23 is not an invitation to individuals to come to Jesus and accept Him into one's life and thereby receive the gift of God which is eternal life. But, it is a declaration of God, that although death was brought upon all through sin entering the human race through Adam, that the gift of God which is eternal life through Jesus Christ replaces the death sentence which was upon all. I Corinthians 15:22, "as in Adam ALL die, in Christ ALL are made alive" —not just physically alive since they already are that but eternally alive through Jesus Christ.

The whole purpose of the sacrifice of Jesus Christ is so that all sin of all time would be paid for by His precious blood of Redemption. Through this act of sacrifice all things in heaven and in earth, humans and the whole cosmos are Reconciled in Jesus Christ. In effect what we see happening is that what Satan, Sin and Adam did were

UNDONE in Jesus Christ as ALL things were RECONCILED in Jesus. (Colossians 1:19-22).

This act of Jesus' Reconciliation applies to all human beings who the scriptures call "The Elect". (Rev.13:8). When we look at Ephesians 1:1-14, we see that Triune God purposed this election and adoption in Jesus Christ before the foundation, or creation, of the world. John 3:16 tells us that "God so loved the world"—the elect—all humanity—everyone "that He sent His only begotten son" to make all the provisions and THE SACRIFICE to seal the deal for God. For us it is matter of Belief.

Before man was ever created we all were adopted and included in the life of Triune God --through Jesus by the Spirit -- before we were even born of our physical mothers. We were "born from above" before we were "born from below"! We were found in Christ before we were 'lost' in Adam. Here is the "mathematical" equation of sin and salvation.

$$Satan+Adam+Sin=DEATH$$

$$+ JESUS\ CHRIST = ETERNAL\ LIFE$$

The plan stands completed in Jesus Christ. It is Finished. Triune God is Victorious.

The Father's Power will continue to see this plan fulfilled in Jesus for ALL.(I Pet.1:3-5).

WHAT IS THE "HELL" OF II PETER 2:4?

II Peter 2:4-9, poses an interesting question for those who believe in a hell fire stance on hell for humans. But, what are these verses actually talking about? Well, let's see.

Peter is at the end of his ministry. He knows he is facing martyrdom. (II Peter 1:14-15). He foresees in the future trouble for the church and warns the church in a number of areas. False prophets, departing from the faith, remaining unentangled from the world, etc. He gives the illustration in II Peter 2 of how God did not "spare" or overlook or ignore it when the angels sinned, but cast them down to "hell". A note here on the words hell is translated from. There are four words in scripture translated by our one word hell. Sheole in the Hebrew meaning **grave** or **pit** appears 65 times in the O.T. Hades meaning **grave** in the Greek appears 11 times in the N.T. Gehenna in the Greek is a trans-language word for the Hebrew word "Hinnom". The valley of Hinnom was a garbage dump outside of Jerusalem where refuse, dead carcasses of animals, garbage, dead derelict humans were thrown, the fires were kept burning, where the smoke continually billowed up, and where flies continually bred with maggots or worms that never died out. The stench was beyond description. Now the last word translated hell.

The word translated hell in II Peter 2:4 is none of these. It is "tartaroo". It means a place of restraint, or imprisonment, or dungeon, or a chaining up. Peter uses the word to explain that this imprisonment on the earth of the angels that sinned was their place of restraint until their judgement time came (vs. 4 and vs. 9), and that **their** punishment would continue until that time. What Peter is saying in the context of II Peter 2 and II Peter 3 is that God is not going to "spare" or overlook the deeds of evil men and false prophets any more than He overlooked the angels that sinned. Their judgment is sure as well. Peter also is saying through these verses that God knows how to deliver Godly men from the snares of evil influences and heresies also.

A key factor in understanding II Peter 2 is to realize that II Peter 3 must be read in conjunction with it. Peter concludes II Peter with the encouragement in II Peter 3:17-18, "... now you know these things so don' t be carried away with the error or heresy of lawless men and stumble, but, Vs. 18, 'Grow in the grace and knowledge of our Lord and savior Jesus Christ.' ".

II Peter 2:4-9 then has nothing to do with any humans being cast down into "hell" or tartaroo or restraint until they are judged, but is referencing the one third of the angels, along with Satan, which left their first estate and are imprisoned on the earth until their judgment. These are the same spirits we wrestle against spiritually in our life as Ephesians chapter 6 mentions.

WILL GOD PUNISH THE WICKED FOREVER?

Western Christianity has been heavily influenced by Roman civil law and the laws of the Old Covenant both with their attendant requirements for PUNISHMENT for certain acts which judicially speaking were fitting for the crimes committed. We carry this concept with us as we approach an understanding of life after death for those who refuse to accept and believe their inclusion in the life of Jesus. We see these "wicked" as having to serve out an eternal condemnation by God to "pay" for their sinful lifestyle on this earth.

Justice DEMANDS punishment. All judicial systems have various sentences for certain crimes which the defendant must pay by serving due time-- up to life in prison.

Since we come at an understanding of how God deals with the wicked after death based on Roman civil law and Old Covenant judgements we understand from a law, punishment, judgement, and payment approach.

When we look at all humans—us included—we see humanity subject to DISOBEDIENCE and in total rebellion against God's laws and principles. Actually God made us this way subject to disobedience so that He could have MERCY on ALL.(Rom.11:32).

The good news is that while we ALL were ungodly sinners in rebellion and hatred against God Christ died for US ALL.(Rom.5:6-8). Christ PAID the Eternal price for all of our sins and wickedness and evilness and ungodliness and suffered all the suffering that is eternally needed or required for all humans. There does NOT

REMAIN any more suffering or punishment or sacrifice that is required by any of us. Christ paid it ALL for ALL for ALL time!

When we come to the question will the wicked be tormented and or punished by God eternally in a state or condition or a place called "Hell", the answer should be OBVIOUS to all of us which is: NO, they will not be dealt with by God since God has already dealt with the ungodly in the suffering and Death of JESUS CHRIST.

What we are talking about here is the EXTREME Grace of God extended to all of His children from the creation of the world. God has taken up all of humanity to His side in Jesus Christ. There is no longer any payment for the sins and wickedness and ungodliness of mankind due. It has been paid in FULL by Jesus Christ. We need to come to a greater understanding of God's LIMITLESS Grace and Total Love demonstrated to us in that while were "yet ungodly sinners" Christ died for us ALL. Now the only question remains: Will individuals believe this TRUTH? To those who do believe they will spend an eternal life in the most joyous fashion possible.

For those, however, who do NOT believe this TRUTH they will spend that same after life in a very different manner or until they do come to belief, repentance or 'metanoia.'. Their existence will be outside the gates of the Holy City. (Rev.22:17). Misery, suffering, weeping and gnashing of teeth, in darkness and very extreme unhappiness. Notice: This will be by their choice due to their choosing NOT to BELIEVE!!!!!!! Note: God is not the one putting them outside the gates. They by their own choice put themselves in that state.

So belief becomes of paramount importance. Our future is secured in Jesus Christ and IN the life of the Great Triune God. Will YOU believe it?

God wants to know if YOU will believe it or not?

HELL. NOT WHAT YOU MAY HAVE THOUGHT

People are 'hell bent' on hanging on to their ever-loving Hell Fire of Punishment and Torment for sinners who they think are not saved. We all grew up with the concept of Hell and Heaven with Hell being the place people were consigned to for living less than moral and perfect lives or who did not measure up spiritually. Hell was a bad, bad place to be sent upon death. An Eternity of 'hot flames' licking our bodies with unimaginable pain, anguish and suffering…forever. FOREVER. How could we believe anything else in our Christian walk? Our parents held Hell over our heads. Preachers held Hell over our heads. Even our own mind held Hell over our own heads!

The question to ask, is where is the loving God the Father of the Bible when all this Hell is going on for all eternity? For most of us this is all too easy to see and understand and believe. We hang on to this 'theology' because it speaks to bad people—really bad people. Humans like Hitler, and Mussolini, and others of the same persuasion. We certainly don't want people like that in heaven with us so the only alternative is HELL. We require "JUDGEMENT" for these people and other bad people as well. Judgement is right. Fair. Equitable. Suffering for suffering. Punishment for sins and evil. Well, you get the picture.

Could it be that this whole picture is not scriptural? Could it be that this whole picture has its origins, not in the Bible, but in the pagan mind of Plato of ancient Greece? For four hundred years before

Christ Plato's concept of an ever burning and torturing hell endured. Could this be true?

Then in the 5th Century A.D. a church leader by the name of Augustine of Hippo, St. Augustine, perpetuated Plato's hell doctrine in the Christian church because he saw that this 'fear tactic' helped keep Christians in line and away from sin. Some sins were classified as 'venial'—which weren't all that bad, but others were classified as 'mortal sins' and they were very bad, so bad in fact that the person committing them had to GO STRAIGHT TO HELL upon death. And SUFFER. FOREVER.

When we understand that the Great Triune God planned our Adoption through Jesus Christ BEFORE THE CREATION OF THE WORLD (Ephesians 1:3-14), and that Jesus Died for ALL mankind from the foundation of the world (Revelation 13:8), and that Jesus' sacrifice was the payment for ALL mankind's sins (I John 2:2), and that Jesus Christ has reconciled the whole of creation and ALL of mankind to Himself (Colossians 1:20), then maybe we need to rethink what hell really is.

We are created in Jesus to live with Him forever in RELATIONSHIP. We belong to Him. He has prepared a joyful and beautiful eternal existence and relationship for us and with us that cannot be described in earthbound terms. When we see this and realize who we are IN Jesus we can act like who we really are.

HELL: When we deny who we are in Jesus or continue living not knowing who we are in Jesus we can live out of our fallenness in Adam and continue suffering, or as scripture says, PERISHING, until such time as we believe who we really are in Jesus.

The sad thing is that we being free moral agents can choose to NEVER accept and believe who we are in Jesus and continue suffering and perishing from now on, even forever. And some might just call that hell.

"I NEVER KNEW YOU!"
MATTHEW 7:21-24

God loves us all unconditionally. No stipulations. No requirements. Not anything. He loves us from before the foundation of the world and wants to be with us forever. His total and complete Grace was extended to us individually in Jesus Christ before we were even born! Our sins were forgiven, we were redeemed, we were reconciled, and we were saved in Jesus before we started our human walk through life. We did not get a say so or a vote. We have ascended with Jesus to the Father's right hand in the heavenly realm and have been seated there with Jesus. (Ephesians 2:6).

With this being said, how would verses such as Matthew 7:21-24 be explained? (see text). The kingdom of Heaven is first and foremost a relationship with God through acceptance and belief in Jesus Christ. Jesus said that the kingdom was here and among us presently. Jesus wants a relationship with all of us and to give us all the abundant life he offers. Acceptance and belief of WHO we are IN Jesus is critical for this to be experienced.

When scripture speaks of Jesus not knowing these people it means He has not known them in the right relationship based on their unbelief and lack of trust in Him. People have "prophesied" or preached in His name, people have driven demons out of others, and miracles have been performed. But, these people doing these things have done them out of personal talent and ability and in some cases with the aid of Satan and even with the help of the Holy Spirit. However, most importantly, they have done so for wrong personal motives and personal exaltation, which did not glorify Jesus, nor did they accept and believe WHO they were in Jesus. They trusted in themselves and not Jesus. It is **they** who never 'knew' Jesus. These people were adopted and included in the life of God from before the foundation of the world like everyone else. (Ephesians 1). Yet, for whatever reason they did not have the relationship of belief and trust in Jesus they needed.

With this kind of self-centered approach to ministering and self-aggrandizement, Jesus is left with no other choice than to say to "get away from me." Jesus calls this kind of action "evil doing". The question is, do they have to stay away from Jesus forever?

God is not willing for any to continue suffering in their own personal mental captivity. He wants all to come to a change of mind about Jesus—what we call repentance. God is very patient and will allow someone all the time necessary to come to this repentance, or 'metanoia, Gk., a change of mind or thinking. When they do and accept who they are in Jesus and believe it they will be blessed by experiencing the abundant life eternally God grants in and through Jesus Christ.

May we All come to see WHO we are in Jesus Christ and Praise His Name for ever.

THE ELECT OF REWARD
OR PUNISHMENT

A common belief today is that God elected or chose some **few** of the created human family to be saved while all the others would be lost and go to hell and burn forever. Said another way, that some would be able to do good works or deeds and "qualify" by their being so holy that God would take them into heaven with Himself and they would live forever with Him. Of course they throw Jesus in the mix to be responsible for those taken to heaven. However, as you will see throughout this book this false reasoning flies in the face of a myriad of scriptures which contradict this thinking. See II Peter 3:9.

Salvation, redemption, reconciliation, adoption and inclusion are not selective but are all **inclusive** for everyone. One scripture is Abraham Lincoln's favorite: I Corinthians 15:22. "As in Adam all die, in Christ ALL are made alive". **Belief** is the key factor for all to experience this life. We will see many more such scriptures throughout this book.

The truth is **no one** is worthy or good enough or holy enough or righteous enough of their own accord to merit heaven and earn all the blessings of the heavenlies. That is why John 14:6 says it this way, Jesus said, "I am the Way, the Truth and the Life. No one comes to the Father except through me." When properly understood, Jesus has taken all of humanity with Himself in resurrection to the right hand of the Father (Ephesians 2:6) and we have all been given New Birth through the resurrection of Jesus. (I Peter 1:3 -6). With this understanding in mind, where could any kind of eternal torment, ie. "hell", exist? When we examine Revelation 21 and 22 we will see the difference between those 'inside' the Holy City and those 'outside' Her gates and what they all are doing. God is not **willing** for any to perish but for all to come to repentance. Repentance (Gk. Metanoia- a chance of mind). (II Peter 3:9). The metanoia is a change of mind as to **Who** we are in Jesus! We see Jesus as our life (Colossians 3:4) and we see that all things were created **in, by, for and through** Jesus. (Colossians 1). Nothing can take man out of Jesus' hands. John 10:28-30.

ARE SET FREE CHRISTIANS FREE TO SIN?

"You shall know the truth and the truth shall set you free." So said Jesus in John 8:32. But when you look around at many Christians who carry guilt, shame, resentments, bitterness, anxiety, insecurity, lack of assurance, and fear, we have to ask oneself what kind of 'truth' is it that they are experiencing? Jesus' words are true to be sure.

Some people see Jesus' words of being set free as a blank check to go out and sin all they want. Free to do whatever whenever they want. They see it as being set free to live under grace in any way they carnally desire. But Jesus gives no one such license to sin freely by being set free. Living under Grace is no permission to sin.

As the offspring of Adam we all live and experience life in the fallen condition bequeathed to us by Adam due to his disobedience. With the influence of Satan the Devil who is the prince of the power of the air and the god of this present world we constantly are bombarded by his spiritual arrows of sin and rebellion. We live with our minds ever telling us that we are weak, sinful, immoral, not spiritual enough, not good enough, not righteous enough, not humble enough, not liked and not loved by God and condemned. And that we probably are going to "hell" since we realize how unworthy we are. We say we are a pretty sorry lot as a whole. And we buy into this. We are literally held in a state of 'captivity' by the sway and influence and power of the Devil. We are Captives. We are NOT FREE!!!

When Jesus says in John 10:10, that 'He came that we might have life and have it more abundantly', He is referencing the freedom of life in knowing Him and what He gives.

Isaiah had prophesied of this freeing of the captivity of humans who were held captive. Isaiah says it this way in Isaiah 61:1, "The Spirit of the Sovereign Lord is on me, because the Lord has anointed me to preach good news to the poor. He has sent me to bind up the broken hearted, to proclaim FREEDOM for the captives and release from darkness for the prisoners, to proclaim the year of the Lord's favor." Jesus quotes this passage of Isaiah in Luke 4:16 word for word. Jesus says that this prophecy is fulfilled at that day and time! The prison was not a physical one but a MENTAL/SPIRITUAL one.!

We were chosen in Christ and Adopted as His children even 'Before the foundation of the world'. Or, before ANYTHING was ever created in the first place!!! (Ephesians 1:3-14; II Timothy 1:9). This truth tells us that while we were yet and still sinners Christ died for us. (Romans 5:8). That all of our sins are forgiven in Christ who is the payment-propitiation-the atoning sacrifice- for our sins and for the sins of the whole world. (I John 2:2). That for those in Christ Jesus there is NO MORE CONDEMNATION. (Romans 8:1). Romans 8:2, goes on to say that through Christ the law of the Spirit of life set me free from the law of sin and death! Christ releases all of us from ANY claim the law ever had on us! We are set free.

Far from giving license to sin all one wants the Christian living chapters of Ephesians 4, Colossians 3, and Romans 12, give guidance as to how one should be living once he or she sees that their life is hidden in Christ and that He is their life. (Colossians 3:4).

But we are **still** sinners. We still sin. Yes, we live in a body of sin and death waiting to be changed from mortal to immortal in the bodily resurrection. (I Corinthians 15). But while we wait we live by the Faith of Jesus Christ in a perpetual state of forgiveness --always clean, always righteous (Romans 3:21), always saved and always loved by our Father in Heaven.

The person who is set free through the Truth, WHO is JESUS, now lives in peace, joy, security, assurance, hope, abundance, and in the love relationship with Jesus Christ. The Father, Holy Spirit and Jesus, The Triune God lives in the individual and the individual LIVES IN the Father, Holy Spirit, and Jesus. (John 17:20-26).

The individual has been freed, set free from all the lies the Devil has devoured him with. The eyes are opened. He sees through the eyes of Faith. The individual is now free to experience the life of God on a personal and loving basis. And this will grow throughout the individuals life by allowing more and more of the mind of Christ to be active in him. (Philippians 2:5).

One final thought. When we sin and we will, we always have a Savior who never counts those sins against us. Never takes note of them. Never remembers them and removes them from us as far as the East is from the West. We just stay forever clean in His eyes through the Word which He has spoken. (John 15:3). We are forever forgiven!

What a FRIEND we have in Jesus Who is the Way, the TRUTH, and the LIFE. Once we know the Truth we are forever set FREE.

DO SCRIPTURES CONTRADICT
THE GOSPEL?

Just wait a minute!!! What about the scripture that says, ...this, that, or the other thing which 'contradicts' what is being said about Trinitarian Theology and the Adoption, Inclusion, and Salvation in **hope** of ALL mankind? There are numerous ones which don't seem to reconcile with this understanding of Theology. The question to ask is Who is doing the reconciling and what criteria is being used?

Are different paradigms being used? Are Augustinian, Calvin, or Armenian theologies being used to interpret the Gospel, or do we interpret with certain 'Absolutes' being given and established from the start? All varying interpretations will only serve to confuse a right understanding of the Gospel.

So, when looking at some scriptures which seem to oppose Trinitarian Theology, we must ask ourselves where do we start in our understanding? We must start with the beginning!

We start with God! The Eternal Father, Son, and Holy Spirit. The Triune God. The Trinity. We start with Jesus who is the Word who has always existed and who is God.(Jn.1:1). "In the beginning was the Word and the Word was with God and was God"

Then we go next to Triune God's 'blueprint' plan. Gen.1:26-27. Here God desires to create humankind in order to share His abundant Love and Divine Nature (II Peter 1:4) which God has existed in as Father, Son, and Holy Spirit Eternally. And, not just creating 'creatures' to have physical life only, but humans to be **adopted** into the very life of God. We see this purpose in Ephesians

1:3-14. Vs.4-5, tell us that it was God's purpose **before** the creation of the world to choose us in Jesus Christ and to **adopt** us AS HIS SONS and DAUGHTERS according to His pleasure and His WILL.

This original plan of God was fully accomplished in Jesus Christ as He came into human existence as Immanuel and created the Union between God and man. As Jesus said describing the Union in John 14:20, "...you will realize that I am IN my Father, and you are IN me, and I am IN you."—UNION. Jesus repeats this truth in John 17:20-26 in His last prayer on earth!!!

As far as the sin question goes, Jesus took care of that for all of mankind by going to the cross and shedding His blood which provides forgiveness for all of humanity and the sins of the world. (I Jn.2:2).

Paul says it this way, "In Adam all die, but in Jesus ALL are made alive." (I Cor.15:22). And in Romans 5:18-19, Paul emphasizes, "that just as the result of one trespass was CONDEMNATION for All men, so also the result of one act of righteousness was justification that brings LIFE for ALL men."

Since we are IN Jesus by His divine act and appointment whatever happened/happens to Jesus also happened/happens to us as well. Jesus died. We are crucified with Him and we died. (Ga.2:20) Jesus rose. We rose. Jesus ascended and we ascended to the right hand of the Father. (Eph.2:6).

What we are describing here is what **has** happened in GOD'S Theology. Of course our physical change into spirit is yet to occur. But it is a done deal with God. It is His music the symphony of life is playing.

The kicker, however, is that man with his free will has the option **not** to believe what God has done in Jesus for his benefit. Man can deny and continue to deny his divine relationship with God. And, man **can** continue to do so **for ever** if he chooses.

Now we come to scriptures which seem to contradict Adoption and Inclusion Theology.

They must be viewed in light of THE LIGHT of the world— Jesus. Viewed in light of what has been said above concerning **God's Will** and **God's Plan.**

Everyone, all humans, all who ever lived are the ADOPTED SONS AND DAUGHTERS OF GOD and have a place reserved in the eternity of heaven for them.(Jn.14) But, here again, all might not experience that heavenly homecoming or party or existence by their own CHOICE by DENYING WHO THEY ARE IN JESUS.

So, we can say that possibly not all will experience eternity in the same way. Most will experience it 'Gloriously' while others will experience it in a MISERABLE, SAD, and ALIANATED condition **outside the gates of the Holy City.** (Revelation 22:17).

The concept of a torturous, fiery, ever burning damning Hell Fire is an idea which was originated by the Greek philosopher Plato in the 400's BC. The concept came into the Christian church through Augustine in the 5th Century AD in order to keep church members in line through fear. It remains current teaching in the Catholic Church today and many Protestant churches as well. It is not a theologically sound and Biblical teaching. (You may want to study this understanding in greater detail, i.e. Lazarus and the rich man, etc.).

A word study would be helpful in various passages showing God's 'indignation' towards the CHOICE some make as to their belief in Jesus. God's eternal perspective towards even those who choose not to believe and who experience continued alienation is still one of LOVE. God is love. He was Love. He is love. He will always be love. He doesn't EVER, EVER, EVER, EVER hate His children. His indignation and anger are directed at their WRONG choices, but His love for the individual still remains. Hence, the POSSIBILITY that eventually those making wrong choices may change their mind, repent and assume their heavenly reward. (Luke 15 and the Prodigal son parable indicates this concerning the older brother as a possibility; See Revelation 22:17). Much more can be said on this topic.

Hopefully this will give perspective on scriptures as you find them, which seem to mitigate against the proper and Godly vision of Trinitarian Theology—simply called THE GOSPEL.

The key for all interpretation of scripture is to answer the question, "WHO IS JESUS?" When we get this question and answer correct then we can proceed to answer all other questions relating to Theology.

DO SOME 'NOT' BELONG
TO CHRIST?
(Or Do All Belong To Christ?)

In this paper let's look at one of the most used verses in all of the Bible to try and discredit or disprove a position of Trinitarian Theology which says that ALL humanity is IN Jesus Christ and that ALL are Adopted (Ephesians 1:5) and ALL are Included in the life of God by the Spirit.(John 14:20).

This verse is Romans 8:9. Specifically 9b which alludes to someone who "has not the Spirit of Christ is none of His." Some would use this verse to try and undo all the other verses which demonstrate that we all belong to Christ.

It is helpful to read ALL of Romans chapters 1-8 to see what Paul is addressing to the Christians at Rome. Paul declares that ALL have sinned and come short of the Glory of God. (Rom.3:23). And that there is no difference between Jews, Gentiles, Christians, non-Christians. (Rom.2:11, "God does not show favoritism."). Paul is writing therefore to EVERYONE for ALL have fallen short of the Glory God.

In Romans 5:18, Paul writes that "the result of one act of righteousness was justification that brings life for ALL men." This act of Jesus 'trumps' the condemnation which was brought upon ALL men by Adam. This life Jesus brought was 'signed, sealed, and delivered' by His LIFE, DEATH, RESURRECTION, AND ASCENSION. And this LIFE was for All descendants of Adam!! EVERYONE.

Back to Romans 8. Paul is simply comparing two ways of life a person can choose to live. One is out of conforming to the dictates and desires of the FLESH, and the other is to yield to the Spirit of Christ within everyone thereby walking or living and being motivated by the Spirit of Christ within.

Verse 9 begins by pointing out that these Romans are no longer **controlled** in life by their sinful nature (flesh) but now knowing WHO THEY ARE IN JESUS are now able to live motivated by the Spirit of Jesus living within them. Paul says that if anyone does not have the Spirit of Christ, he is none of His. Paul is not saying that there are some who don't, he is pointing out that since All things BELONG to Christ obviously they belong and they DO have Christ's Spirit and therefore they ARE Christ's.

Verse 10 makes it more plain. "But SINCE…(ei, in the Greek and here in vs.10 is what is referred to in the Greek language as' a first class conditional clause which assumes that the statement which follows is TRUE, therefore Since should be used here and not if. Since and if are both translated from "ei" in the Greek. (see Colossians 2:20)…Christ IS IN you, your body is dead because of sin, yet your spirit is alive because of righteousness—Jesus' righteousness declared to us! Paul knows what he is talking about.

There are only two ways to live. One is not to know who we are IN Jesus and walk according to the fallen, sinful, flesh we possess, and the other is to know we belong to Jesus, believe we belong to Jesus, and behave and live our life out of the Spirit of Jesus which lives in us ALL. One is called walking after the flesh, and the other is called walking and living after the Spirit—motivated by grace and the Spirit. The question then is what is **motivating** our life?

When one realizes Who he or she is in Jesus and believes it and lives accordingly then Jesus can claim this individual as ONE OF HIS who is a BELIEVER. Those who live in Jesus but who are non-believers still belong to Jesus but they are NONE OF HIS BELIEVERS-----YET! Remember ALL things were and are created IN Jesus, By Jesus, Through Jesus, and FOR Jesus and are upheld and sustained BY Jesus. (Colossians 1:16-17). Obviously All humanity belongs to Jesus and are His.

Paul is not going to claim a spiritual fact in one book of his only to nullify it in another. He does not speak out of 'both sides of his mouth'.

There are other verses such as this we have discussed here that seem to contradict the Gospel. However, when understood in LIGHT of the LIGHT OF THE WORLD--JESUS, they become much more clear.

GOD HAS FULLY BLESSED
US ALL IN JESUS

What do you think of when you hear the words Blessings of God? The health wealth babblers would have us to believe that God will "bless" us with bountiful incalculable riches and abundance in response to our 'giving' to him our offerings and our 'seed' money. But are the blessings of God something that are future for us? And if they are what could they possibly be? What do I mean by all of this?

Let's see. What are the greatest blessings that could possibly be poured out and or given to man by our loving Father in Heaven? James 1:17 gives us insight into God's giving nature and His sharing heart when James says that "every good and perfect gift is from above coming from the Father." But are these gifts God gives something future based on how we perform, or what we do or don't do, or based on some kind of work we may do or even on our faith?

In answering these questions we need to go to Ephesians Chapter 1 and notice carefully what Paul is saying to **all** of us. Eph.1:3, Paul says for Praise to be given to God the Father of our Lord Jesus Christ who HAS BLESSED us in the heavenly realms—or with the 'Treasures of Heaven'—with EVERY spiritual blessing in Christ! What Paul is saying here is that God has ALREADY, PAST ACTION, PAST TENSE, blessed us all with the Treasures of Heaven and with every spiritual blessing that it is possible to give and it is all done in the person of Jesus Christ!

There could be much discussion as to what all these Blessings are, but a better understanding of verse 4 here will shed a little more light on the subject. Vs. 4, "For He chose us in Him before the creation of the world to be holy and blameless in His sight…" Holy and blameless in His sight here would better be rendered, "to be face to face in intimate relationship with God." This is how the Father, Son, and Holy Spirit are in relationship. They are "face to face". Intimate. Relational. Loving. When John speaks of the Word being 'with' God in the beginning in John 1:1, 'with' doesn't mean side by side like three statues of some sort like relics in a museum, but FACE TO FACE. Divine Loving INTIMACY. And this is how God chose us to be IN Him before the foundation of the world. Triune God wants to SHARE this love relationship With us, in us, and we in Him/Them. Jesus phrases it this way in John 14:20, the Heart of the Gospel, that the Spirit will reveal to you this, "On that day you will realize that I am IN my Father, and you are IN me, and I am IN you." It is all a matter of the Intimacy God has desired from the start of this plan of His. Unfortunately some have looked at verse 4 from a very legalistic, morally straight, squeaky clean understanding of what it means to be 'holy and blameless in His sight and have missed the beautiful relational aspect of the Triune God and our Inclusion **in** that relationship. Triune God does not exist in a structured, law defining, legalistically calculable three in one and one in three sterile grand state. They exist in RELATIONSHIP, IN LOVE, IN HONOR, IN RESPECT, IN INTIMACY Face to Face!

We humans have no need to look for any greater blessing ever in all of eternity than the BLESSINGS God has ALREADY GIVEN to us in Jesus Christ. If we have been given the 'Treasures of Heaven' and every Spiritual blessing in Christ—PAST TENSE—what more could possibly be given to us now or in the future.

What we are looking for in our life now and forever is how to enjoy and experience these FANTASATIC Blessings God has in His loving heart already given to us. Eph.1:4- 6, "In God's great Love He predestined us to be ADOPTED as His sons/and daughters through Jesus Christ in accordance with His Pleasure and His Divine Will to the praise of His Glorious Grace which He has FREELY GIVEN US IN THE ONE HE LOVES". Vs.7, shows how this can happen to all of us fallen, pitiful, sinful, wicked humans. "In Him we have REDEMPTION through His blood the forgiveness of sins in accordance with the RICHES—unbelievable RICHES—of God's GRACE that He LAVISHED on us." More and more of an understanding of God's Great Love for us should come clearer to all of us when we really realize what God has actually done For all of us and To all of us in Jesus Christ.

The awesome thing to comprehend is that all of this was done BERORE THE FOUNDATION OF THE WORLD, BEFORE CREATION. BEFORE ADAM! AND BEFORE TIME. (Ephesians 1:3-6; II Timothy 1:9). And God planned it all this way so that it had His GUARANTEE of Success on it before it ever started. Done. Done Deal. Victory. Jesus said, "It is Finished", and it was, before it ever got started to begin with!!! The only question remains is, "Will a person accept this and believe it?" I pray all will.

GOD'S ORIGINAL PLAN
STANDS FIRM FOREVER

Let's make the Plan of God and the Gospel, the GOOD NEWS really simple. After all, it isn't rocket science! We are the ones who have made a manmade gospel. Man has made man far too important in the salvation process with far too much dependence on his salvation placed on man.

Originally when Triune God decided to share His love with a creation and with His created children He is the one who devised the plan with all contingencies to make absolutely sure that plan would follow through to completion.

God planned to create man and send His Son, the Word, to become human and bridge the gap between God and man so that man could live in Union with the Father, Son, and Holy Spirit inside of God's life FOREVER. To ADOPT man into the very life of God.

This is what the All Powerful, Almighty God wanted to do. No matter what happened in the new life of His created children, Adam and Eve, God's Plan would stand secure.

So man was chosen in Christ before the foundation of the world to be Holy in Jesus and to live eternally with God in God's life. (Eph.1:3-15). Jesus had to become human in order to create the "bridge" of humanness into the LIFE of GOD and create that Union, that connection.

God knew, however, that when Adam sinned that would pose a problem that needed a fix so that God's original plan could continue on and man would still be headed to eternal life and existence in the original plan God had from beginning.

We read in Rev.13:8, that Jesus was slain before the foundation of the world. So we see that God chose humanity IN Jesus before the foundation of the world and foresaw that Adam (man) would sin and bring the death penalty on all of his descendants thereby necessitating the need for a sacrifice for man's sins and a Savior that only Jesus could provide. That eventuality was planned for and taken care of in Jesus. In other words, Jesus undid what Adam did! Jesus corrected the problem. He CONQUERED the problem.

God wanted man in His Life from beginning. God being all powerful and all-knowing and all loving was not going to let sin and Satan thwart His eternal plan and purpose for man. Jesus would fix or "undo" what Adam did by Adam's sinning.

We read in I Cor. 15:22, that in Adam ALL die, so IN Jesus Christ ALL—the SAME All--are made ALIVE. We could look at it this way. God's plan from the beginning started. It was proceeding along very well. Adam sinned and took mankind OFF of the track, but Jesus put man BACK on the track, took all responsibility for the sins, life, death, new birth, resurrection and ascension of man by becoming human in the incarnation, living a perfect life, and QUALIFYING all humanity to live in God's presence and **IN** God's life forever just as was originally planned by The TRIUNE GOD.

God further states this fact in Romans 8:31-39. What happened with Adam by the influence of Satan is NOT going to happen again! Jesus took care of that possibility. God's plan and purpose stands. It is His Good Pleasure to give us His Kingdom and Life. (Luke 12:32).

"It is Finished", Jesus said. He is the Alpha and Omega. The beginner and finisher of our faith. He is the originator and perfector of our faith. It is ALL in His hands. All creation was created in and by and for and through Jesus Christ. And, He sustains that creation. It is HIS. Jesus has done EVERYTHING to ASSURE The Great God's Plan is fulfilled and completed.

God's desire has always been to take man into the Life of God forever. And nothing can ever change that REALITY. (Rom.8:31-39). And why? "For God so loved the world…"

IS GOD DISTANT AND UNINVOLVED

You are aware of most people's view of God: Distant. Disconnected. Non-involved with His creation. Jesus talked about His Loving Father and the Triune existence of God that is in human beings. (John 14:20; John 17:20-26). The early church leaders talked about Adoption and Inclusion in the life of God. Men like Paul, John, Polycarp, Irenaeus, Athanasius, and others wrote of this truth. So how did we come to view God in the 21st Century the way most Christians do as distant and uninvolved?

Just prior to the Reformation in the 1600's great church leaders such as John Calvin, Martin Luther, and others were seeing the great truth of the Triune existence of God in humanity and His connection to His creation. But something monumental was happening in the world of thought that eclipsed the theological thinking of the Reformation.

The European world had been dominated by the Church during the lower and Middle Ages. The time was ripe for a change in thinking and attitudes. Partly as a backlash against the tyranny of the Church and the domination of politics extant in the world, great thinkers emerged with what came to be known as the "Enlightenment". Or, the Enlightenment of Reason, or the Age of Reason. This dramatic change in thinking occurred from the 17th Century on through the 18th. The faith in the church was hijacked by this revolution in thinking. Where God had been central in theological thinking, now reason, intelligence, philosophy, invention, mechanics, politics and science would replace God in man's view of 'authority'. The saviour of man would now be man and his intellect with no real need for God.

Famous men of the Enlightenment, just to name a few, included Rene Descartes, Edmund Burke, Edward Gibbon, David Hume, Immanuel Kant, Thomas Jefferson, John Locke, Montesquieu, Thomas Paine, Voltaire, Rousseau, and Isaac Newton.

The Enlightenment religion of the day became what is known as DEISM, from the Latin word deus meaning god. Deism emphasized reason. It believed in one God as creator of the cosmos, but was opposed to revelation and the thought that God dwelt in man or was continuously active in the affairs of the world. Or to put it another way, God created the cosmos and the world and wound it up like a giant clock, turned it on, and let it go on its own. So after creating the cosmos God just walked away.

This "religion" essentially did away with God as Frederic Nietzsche would say, "God is dead." Man could now do as he pleased with no restraints from a God who was distant and uninvolved. Romans 1:20-25 describes what reasonings are behind this kind of thinking!

But the Enlightenment and the Deism which pervaded the period were not the finishing blow to the faith of the church. That esteemed honor came to a refined, educated Englishman and graduate of Cambridge University, Charles Robert Darwin.

Darwin published his Origin of the Species in 1859 which formed the basis for the evolutionary thought which would push the creator completely out of the cosmic picture. Although Darwin did not specifically write defining the evolution of humans, only plants and animals, his assumptions and theories were expanded by others to mean the evolution of man from lower forms in the anthropological assent to humans. The world today continues to suffer under these false concepts and God remains distant and uninvolved.

But what is the Truth? We read in Colossians 1:16-17; Ephesians 1:22; Hebrews 1:3, that Jesus Christ is the Creator and that All things were created BY and THROUGH, and IN, and FOR Jesus AND that He SUSTAINS or UPHOLDS ALL THINGS.

Jesus said that the Kingdom is among us. Jesus said that He and Father and the Holy Spirit would make their home IN us. And for Jesus to uphold all things and sustain all things, He must be in all things.

Paul said in Acts 17:28 when debating with the pagans at Athens that, "we live, and move, and have our being in the Creator God."

Jesus is the 'Light of the world'. That light has not gone out and did not go out with the Enlightenment and the philosophy of Deism. Not only is Jesus the light of the world, John says in John 1:4 that in Him was/is LIFE. There is no life apart from the source of life which is the indwelling life of Jesus in all living things. After all, He did breathe the breath of life into all living-breathing creatures! Ecclesiastes 3:19-21 speaks of this breath and spirit of life in animals and beasts.

God knows when a sparrow falls to the ground. He is in it and there. (Luke 12:6). We are told in Psalm 148 and in Psalm 8 for all the creation to praise God. God is very much in His creation. His life permeates all living things. His Spirit permeates all of the cosmos. All of the Universe. David said this in Psalm 139:7-12. God swims in and with the whales by His Spirit. He soars with the eagles by His Spirit. His Spirit is alive and in and upholding and sustaining ALL of the Creation.

Our loving Triune God, Father, Son, and Holy Spirit, has desired to share His life and eternity with us His children—FOREVER. He is not far off. He is here and now. He is personal and relational. He LOVES you, always has, always will. And He has made all the provisions for you to be with Him for all eternity in Glory. Can you believe this?

IS JESUS' RESURRECTION
ALL INCLUSIVE?

Jesus makes a profound statement to Martha, Lazarus' sister, in John 11:25. Lazarus has died and four days have passed. Lazarus had been a "good" man and therefore in Jewish Pharisee philosophy would be resurrected at the last day in the resurrection. Martha states this to Jesus in verse 24.

But Jesus makes a POWERFUL statement to Martha when He says, "I AM the resurrection and the life." Let's carry this statement a little further to understand its impact. Jesus is saying, "Here is a situation with Lazarus which will allow me to state just WHO I AM and demonstrate why I have come and that I have the Power to resurrect the dead. So, let me tell you who I am. I am the Incarnate Son of God and I came to rectify the fallenness in Adam of ALL Humanity who are DEAD in Adam—Past, Present, and Future—and to be THE RESURRECTION and THE LIFE for ALL Humanity and raise ALL people up in my Resurrection thus bridging the gap between God and man thereby creating UNION between God and man. I am the source and the ONLY source for ALL of humanity to be resurrected. Let me begin to show this power to resurrect now by raising Lazarus."

Matthew continues this theme in Matthew 27:50-53. This is the account After the Resurrection of Jesus when the graves in and around Jerusalem were opened and the DEAD came up in resurrection. This demonstrated again God's power to raise the dead. But it was also a FORSHADOWING of the Resurrection of ALL of humanity in Jesus in God's time order—Jesus, of course, being the First (I Corinthians 15:23).

In I Corinthians Paul further shows that the resurrection of Jesus Christ and ALL of Humanity's resurrection stand or fall together. If one is not true, then NEITHER is true.

(I Corinthians 15:16). Paul then goes one step further when in verse 22 he says, "For AS in Adam ALL die, SO in Christ ALL WILL be made alive." No one is excluded. Just as no one has ever been excluded or will ever be excluded in dying as a result of Adam. No one is excluded from being made alive IN Jesus Christ. Paul says it this way in Colossians 3:1-4. "...you have been RAISED with Christ. "Christ IS your LIFE."

John tells us in Revelation 13:8 that the Lamb of God was slain from the foundation of the world. When Christ was crucified and died in the early 30's A.D. His blood reached all the way back to Adam and ALL of Adam's descendants and forward to every human being who would ever live in the human family line of Adam. Therefore, ALL are redeemed in the blood of Jesus no matter when they live! There can be NO ONE excluded. And NO ONE is!

Jesus came to seek and to save what was lost, humanity and the creation, and He did. (See (Luke 19:10). Jesus came to reveal Himself as the Resurrection and the Life. See this in (John 11:25). Jesus came to live, die, be resurrected and to ascend to the Father's right hand AND to carry Humanity to the Father's right hand WITH Him by being humanity's life, death, resurrection and ascension. (Ephesians 2:6).

God had a 'lock tight' plan from the very beginning to Adopt and Include humanity into the life of the Triune God—Father, Son, and Holy Spirit. (Ephesians 1:3-14). Throughout the history of man God has NEVER wavered in His Plan for humanity. In Jesus the Plan is complete. "It is finished," Jesus said in John 19:30.

In Jesus the FULLNESS of the Plan will ultimately be REALITY. God WILL wipe away all tears. (Revelation 21:4). Joy and happiness and peace and righteousness will reign in the FULL KINGDOM OF GOD FOREVER.

All of this will be completed because of one man. The man who was fully human and fully God, Jesus Christ. The question is, can we believe this magnificent truth? Can we believe the WORD? Can we believe the Son of God, Jesus Christ?

WE NEVER DIE IN JESUS

Upon one's physical death, does the person continue to live in the presence of God? Some say yes and some say no. Some posit that the person is in the grave in a state of "sleep" awaiting a future resurrection. While scripture is not 'specific' on this subject, there are theological implications which may help us answer the question.

Let us remember that time and space were created by the Triune God. God does not operate confined to His created time. Past, present and future are terms we use to define events in linear time by which God is not governed.

In God's economy of existence He simply is involved in His creation as everything being in the present. Subjectivity and objectivity of understanding obviously are operative here. Without confusing the issue here, Einstein demonstrated that in times space, with time and space being the same thing, that past, present and future were all the same...present. Do I understand that, quite honestly... NO. But then again there is much about the great Triune God I do not understand. Back to the original question.

We see in Genesis 1 that God did not intend for man to die but to continue living. Sin brought the death factor upon Adam and all of his descendants. Now it is appointed man ONCE to die. (Heb.9:27). And humanity has lived in the fear of death since Adam. (Heb.2:14-15).

Jesus shows, however, in John 5:24, that those who believe Him and the Father HAVE ETERNAL LIFE and have crossed over INTO LIFE! Jesus IS their life and the person's life is now hidden with Christ in God. (Col.3:3-4; also, Acts 17:28).

Paul mentions this operation in II Cor.5:1-8, as we who are mortal in our earthly tent may be swallowed up by LIFE. He says to be away from the body is "to be home with the Lord." Then, in Philippians 1:21-24, Paul points out that to die is gain, or an improvement that is much better. Paul does not indicate that this would be anything other than immediate. Simply a change from mortal at death to immortal and life which is in Christ.

We know that we live and move and have our being in Christ. (Acts 17:28). And we know that Christ is our life. And we know that we have passed from death into life. And we know that Jesus conquered and defeated death. And we know that we are resurrected in and with Jesus who is our resurrection. (Col.3:1). Now what Jesus tells Martha in John 11:25-26 has a much clearer meaning. "I am the resurrection and the life, he who believes in me will LIVE (Gk. "Zesetai" is live here and carries the meaning of 'shall continue to live') even though he dies. And whoever lives and believes in me will NEVER die. Do you believe this?" What Jesus is saying, I believe, is that at our mortal body' death we CONTINUE to live in our new existence since Jesus is our life and we participate in His resurrection. (I Peter 1:3). And, therefore, objectively speaking, we are seated at the Father's right hand with Jesus now. (Eph.2:6).

I think we have confused in the past our resurrection as being "OUR" resurrection and not the fact that we have been resurrected in Jesus already. What we are awaiting is the "**resuscitation**" of our mortal bodies to meet up with our resurrected spirit and thereby live in and with God in the heavenlies forever in our new spirit body which will be like Jesus' body now. (ICor.15:49, I Jn.3:2)

In Jesus there simply is no death, no cessation of life. We live and move and have our being IN Jesus Christ and therefore we live eternally with no possibility of death. Death itself does not even separate us from the love of God. We and that love continue on. (Rom.8:37-39).

How we may have looked at scriptures before concerning resurrections (plural) and other events as well was from a linear time and dispensational standpoint we put things in 'order' and sequenced events based on our time frame as we interpreted past events and prophetic writings. While those may seem to have fit, we simply cannot ignore the very words of Jesus Christ as He encourages us with the fact of our NEVER dying again in Him. We have passed from death into life...Forever.

ARE THE DEAD CONSCIOUS WITH GOD NOW?

Are deceased loved ones consciously alive and with God now? Or, are they "soul sleeping" and waiting on the resurrection to be "awake" and with God then? Of course the only ones who are concerned with this question are those of us who are still ALIVE.

Scripture can be taken supporting both perspectives mentioned here. However, most all of the time when this is questioned the perspective is one which involves linear time. Time which is confined to the parameters of time and space—the dimension we live in as humans.

God is not confined to time and space and linear time. God is eternal and in one sense views all things in the present from his vantage point outside of time and space. One theologian said, "God gives us linear time and space so everything doesn't happen at once!"

We know when an individual dies that the spirit goes to God. Some would say that this spirit is immediately conscious with God. Others would say that this spirit is NOT conscious and is awaiting the resurrection to become conscious. One is now, the other is later—however how much later this later is.

But think about it from the deceased person's stance. He or she is dead not knowing anything until they realize they are in God's presence and loving arms I might add. But, whether that length of time is a nano second at death, or 1000 years or a million years, to the individual it is **instantly**. It is like one going to sleep at night then waking up not knowing if he has slept one or two hours or six or seven!

There can be philosophical arguments as to why one way or the other would be more appropriate and many do argue those perspectives.

If the individual enters God's heavenly presence not confined to linear time and space, then no matter how much "time" elapses the individual is immediately conscious and with God at death and therefore how we "calculate" it has no bearing in the matter.

The answer as to how God does this is to say that He does it for the very best of all concerned based on His Unconditional Love for all people.

WHO COMES INSIDE THE "PARTY"?

Revelation poses for us a real problem between Chapter 20 and Chapter 22. For any looking for a literal interpretation of Revelation or a dispensational view of prophecy, there is a situation going on here which is obviously contradictory as far as the eternal fate of some goes.

In Revelation 20:15, "If anyone's name was not found written in the Book of Life, he was thrown into the lake of fire." In verse 14 this is called the "second death". Then in Revelation 21:8, we see a group of individuals which here says they will have their place in the lake of fire, the second death."

Now let's come to Revelation 22:14, "Blessed are those who wash their robes that they may have the right to the tree of life, and may go through the gates into the City (New Jerusalem)." Then verse 15 says that **Outside the city are the dogs, those who practice magic arts, the sexually immoral, the murderers, the idolaters and all liars."**

Revelation 22:12, Jesus says He is going to give to **everyone** according to what he has done. The question here is what is meant by what he has done? Is it what the individual has done in his earthly life? If that is true then entrance into "heaven" or the City of Heaven is based on works!!! What the person did. Then its "here we go again" with the works / grace controversy. Could it be that what Jesus is referring to here in vs. 12 when He says, "I will give to everyone according to what he has done" is a reference to **BELIEVING** Jesus and **Who they are eternally in Jesus.** Here I refer you back to

John chapter 3:18. Belief is connected to not being condemned and unbelief is connected to standing in condemnation—or continued suffering and alienation in their unbelief.

If grace is true, and it is, then what Jesus is saying to **ALL** is that the good thing to do in order to participate in the Eternal Life in the joys of heaven is **TO BELIEVE.** By not believing, ie, not washing their robes **IN JESUS** and believing, they simply remain "unwashed", alienated, perishing, in suffering torment, "outside the city" in what the scripture calls the state of "second death" or lake of fire. Note: But God does not give up on them. See Revelation 22:17—this is outside the gates! They will experience God's love so intense as to be compared to "fire".

When you stop to consider what those INSIDE the City are experiencing compared to what those OUTSIDE the City are experiencing the comparison between what we call **Heaven and hell** seems to become quite a bit clearer.

In conclusion, the place to start in answering any question concerning any scripture is to begin with **WHO IS JESUS?** When we see that the purpose of God has always been.

Adoption into the Triune life of God through Jesus Christ, the scales fall off of our eyes, our vision clears up and we see the glorious Eternal future of **ALL,** both the living and the dead, who ultimately come to see the **TRUTH THAT IS IN JESUS** and **BELIEVE IT.**

God is patient, not willing for any to perish, but for all to come to Repentance or in the Greek, "**METANOIA" Gk —A CHANGE OF MIND AND THINKING--BELIEF. A**nd God is ready to spend an **ETERNITY** helping humans, who have not of yet done so, **wash their robes in Jesus** and enter into the glories of the Father's House and into the party of Heaven.

BEFORE TIME BEGAN

(Enjoy this little outline)

God establishes His Devin Master Plan for His building of His family with no POSSIBILITY OF FAILURE!

1.) Jesus Christ was chosen and slain before the foundation of the world!

I Pt.1:18-21   Christ was chosen before the creation of the world as Saviour.

Rev. 13:8   Christ was slain FROM the creation of the world.

Heb. 2:9   Christ tasted death for every man (from the foundation of the World.)

2.) God CHOSE us INDIVIDUALLY AND PERSONALLY IN CHRIST before the CREATION of the world.

Eph. 1: 4-14   ...He chose us IN Him before the creation of the world to BE (Not BECOME) Holy and Blameless IN His sight, and done so by His glorious Grace and by His Will and for His good pleasure!

II Tim.1:8-10 God's Grace was given to us in Christ before the beginning of time. And now is revealed to us.

II Thes.2:13 ...from the beginning God chose you(me) (by personal name)

81

	To be saved through the sanctifying work of the Spirit and through belief in the truth.
Titus 1:1	God's elect promised eternal life before the beginning of time.
Rom.8: 28–34	God FOREKNEW us and PREDESTINED us to be conformed to the likeness of His Son.

For Christians Salvation is a done deal. And was so from the Foundation of the world. Jesus said in Mt.25:34 to those on His right, "Come inherit the Kingdom prepared for you SINCE THE CREATION OF THE WORLD.

The concept of our Individual predestination by God from the beginning is somewhat foreign to us since we used to say that God only predestined a "family", but not individuals. God did predestinate a Family, and we were chosen to be in it from the foundation of the world.

We truly are a chosen people, I Pt.2: 4–10. Not chosen in the 20th Century by any of our merits, but by God's love and Grace from the beginning.

YOUR PERSONAL GOOD NEWS

Let's just cut to the chase. What you may have heard concerning Christianity, religion, and Theology aside we will look at some astoundingly good news most have never dreamed of.

The great Triune Creator God created human kind in order to share His LIFE of total love with that human family. God adopted humankind into his very life from the very beginning even before the foundation of the world! (Eph.1:3-14). Jesus Christ created everything that exists FOR Himself and He sustains that creation. (Col.1:14-17).

Triune God was so full of love and LIFE that it was bursting to overflow into "something" and that something was the human family God created and started with Adam.

The only way God could experience human life was to become human and in so doing was able to carry humanity into the very heart of Himself. But this union was not one sided. As humanity was carried into the heart of the Triune God, the LIFE, heart, essence, existence, spirit, being of God was imported into humankind by the Spirit of God making the connection, the union between God and man complete. All this was done through Jesus Christ's life, death, resurrection and ascension to the Father.

The GOOD NEWS of the Bible is simply this. We are God's children, with God's Life living in us by His Spirit and loved by our Father. We have an eternal future planned for us in our Father's house with the rest of our brothers and sisters. We can share in the abundance of that life now by knowing about it, knowing where it comes from in Jesus Christ, and believing it.

This is not an "IF" proposition. This is not something "to be" acquired. This is the TRUTH OF GOD. This is an ETERNAL DECLARATION AND PROCLAMATION of the WAY IT IS!

Adam's sin brought untold suffering and death into the human family. But in Jesus Christ abundant JOY and LIFE has replaced that suffering and death. (I Cor. 15:22).

The KEY is understanding what The Triune God's original purpose was and His POWER to bring it all about. (I Peter 1:3-6). And He has! In JESUS CHRIST.

The really good news NOW is that… **YOU ARE INCLUDED** …in the whole plan and you have been since before the foundation of the world. (Eph.1:3-14). And before time! (II Tim.1:9). God has ALWAYS loved **YOU!**

Many QUESTIONS arise over this brief explanation of the Gospel. Some may call it an over simplification. What about this and what about that? What about sin? What about works? What about bad people? What about "Hell"? The "what abouts' are almost endless. But the Good News is Jesus. God With us. God WITHIN us. Immanuel. The answers are to be found to be sure. But they are ONLY found in Jesus. The place to start with any question is, "WHO is JESUS?" When we start there at the correct starting place the beauty of the PLAN OF GOD opens up to our understanding like a beautiful flower on a spring morning.

GOD is LOVE. He loves YOU. You are the SON or DAUGHTER God has always loved and wanted. YOU are SPECIAL to God. How good is that?

And our future as Psalm 16:11 says will be filled "with pleasures forevermore at God's right hand." FOREVER.

You are loved, liked, wanted, adopted and included in the life of God. Jesus made it happen for all of us. Believe it!

ADOPTED AND INCLUDED
IN GOD'S LIFE

The god of this world has deceived it so completely that the truth of God and His love for us as demonstrated from His original plan to take humanity into His very life and live forever with all of us has been all but lost in the religions of the world. (II Cor.4:4).

The Father, Son, and Holy Spirit destined us to be adopted (Ephesians 1:3-5) into the very life of God through the incarnation of the Word which became flesh—Jesus Christ. Whether man ever sinned or not, the plan was going to be completed in Jesus. However, when man did sin all of the sin of the world was taken away in the ultimate sacrifice of the life of Jesus Christ. Sin no longer would factor into the salvation equation for man. Through the one man Jesus life was granted to all humanity. (Romans 5:18; I Cor.15:22-23).

With the incarnation of the Word, God connected humanity and created the necessary UNION to take humanity into God's existence and very life through the Spirit. Jesus talks about this in John 14:20 when He says that, "...in that day you will realize that I am in the Father, you are in me, and I am in you." Later we see in Acts 2 the Holy Spirit being poured out on all people to allow us all to begin to see this reality.

With the life, death, resurrection and ascension of Jesus and His being seated at the right hand of the Father, we were taken by Jesus and seated with Him at the Father's right hand as well. (Spiritually and Objectively speaking, Ephesians 2:6). And blessed with Him as well in the Heavenly realms. (Ephesians 1:3).

The radical truth of this means that in Christ the fullness of the Deity lives in bodily form and that we have been given fullness in Christ. (Colossians 2:9-10). Another way of saying this is to say that The Triune God has taken us INTO His very Triune life by and through Jesus Christ in and by the Spirit. This is WHO we really are and WHERE we really are. FOREVER.

Notice the "Past tense" application of all of this for us. This is not something that is going to happen in the future, this has already happened in Jesus Christ. The Holy Spirit is just revealing it to us more and more and one of these days we will see it in its fullness when we "see Jesus as He is." We will be "like" Him with His likeness. (I John 3:2).

We often mistake I Corinthians 2:9 as being fulfilled in the future. This verse says that no eye has seen, no ear heard, no mind conceived what God has prepared for those who love Him. But verse 10 clearly says that by the Holy Spirit of God He has revealed these things to us NOW.! This is what we are discussing here in this paper. It can't get any better for us all than what you read here. How could you ever add to what God has already done for us, to us, in us, and blessed us with in Jesus and even included us into His very life forever? We just wait for it ALL to be revealed to us in His "time".

INTO THE IMAGE OF GOD

(From a Trinitarian Theological Perspective)

"Let us make man in our image." Genesis 1:26-27. Most have really never thought what this actually means supported by other scriptures. Could it mean more than we have ever thought? This brief outline demonstrates the reality that Triune God has created humanity, not only 'in' His image but **inside** of His very life and existence in order to share His Divine Nature with His children. This has always been His desire and His will and He has accomplished His original plan through the life, death, resurrection and ascension of His Son, Jesus Christ.

To start with, here are a few disclaimers concerning 'hell'.

A. Hell concept totally from PAGANISM. Chinese, Egyptians, Greek religions and in virtually ALL ancient religions except for a very few.
B. Plato gives the Greek underworld the name "hell" @400 B.C.
C. With St. Jerome and St. Augustine in 400's A.D. Hell is introduced by wording into the Latin Vulgate translation. 382 A.D. to 405 A.D.

★★★WHY is this important to know? It mitigates against God's love!!!!!!!

1. God desired to share His divine Love with man ORIGINALLY!
   II Pet. 1:3-4   Share His nature by GREAT PROMISES

Ephesians 1:3-5   Before Creation!

II Tim. 1:9   Before Time

II Cor. 1:18-22   Jesus is the "Yes" to God's promises.

2. In/Into the Image of God
    Gen. 1:26-27 "Let us make man in/into our image.
    Ideas on what this means. "Personality, creativity, Body, Soul, Spirit, etc.
    In/into meaning "inside of" or "within" God's life and existence.
    No physical image, not visible, God is SPIRIT.
    John 14:20 ; John 17:20-23 God lives in us and we IN Him.

3. God is sharing His Divine Nature with us NOW.
    Gal. 5. Fruits of the Spirit

Love	Joy	Faithfulness
Feeling	Peace	Gentleness
Emotion	Patience	Giving
Empathy	Kindness	Sharing
Sympathy	Goodness	Caring

Appreciation for Beauty, Music, Arts, Sunsets/Sunrises

4. Growing into the Image and Likeness of God
    II Cor. 3:18 Growing and transformed into His Likeness and thereby reflecting His Glory!

5. Jesus is the Yes to God's Promises.
    II Cor.1:18-22 Jesus is the YES to all of God's promises.
    John 19:30 It is Finished.

www.Trinitarianletters.com

WHAT THE "LAST" JUDGEMENT IS AND IS NOT

The Last Judgement, or Judgement Day when understood properly gives great relief and encouragement to all. Many, if not most, people have a great fear of being judged by their acts in this life when they give "account" of them at Judgement Day. Most religions have a type of judgement day in their beliefs. Bottom line: If one is judged good enough then reward/heaven; if one is judged bad/evil enough then punishment/purgatory/hell.

It is true that Nineveh, the Queen of the South, and Sodom and Gomorrah will rise in the Judgement of the final day. This of course requires resurrection at some future time. Jesus says in John 12:31, that "now is the time for judgement on this world." Peter says in I Peter 4:17, that "judgement has already started with the family of God."

We know that ALL men/women have been judged guilty in Adam and have received death as a sentence. But, we know that in Jesus Christ those same **ALL** will be made alive in Jesus Christ. We know that all humanity was **chosen** in Christ before the foundation of the world and predetermined to be adopted as sons/daughters through Jesus Christ. (Ephesians 1:4-6). We know that all are included in this plan as John 3:16-17 shows—along with many other verses as well. Titus 2:11 points out that the Grace of God which bequeaths salvation has 'appeared' or is 'applied' to **ALL** men—humanity.

With these realities in mind what can the "Last Judgement" **possibly** be? First, all of humanity has **already** been judged!!! All humans are judged guilty. The wages of sin, which all have committed, is death! (Romans 3:23; Romans 6:23). Now this is where it gets really good. "But the **GIFT** of God is eternal life through Jesus Christ." This eternal life has been given to **ALL HUMAN BEINGS.** This gift extends all the way back to Adam—for ALL. Jesus was slain from the "foundation of the world". (Revelation 13:8). Jesus' sacrifice applies to ALL. (I John 2:2).

So, for humanity, there is no escaping what Jesus has done for all of the sons and daughters of Adam. He has, hold on, **adopted, redeemed, reconciled, forgiven, accepted, liked, loved, saved, included, justified, predestined, glorified, resurrected, and seated at the Father's side ALL OF HUMANITY.** (If you can think of something I left out here, just add it!)

Now back to the "Last Judgement." Whenever in resurrection one stands before the judgement seat of Christ he stands guilty, guilty, guilty. But, he also stands completely forgiven. If he does not know this, then the last judgement is to declare to him that yes he is a sinner and guilty, but that Jesus has taken care of that and forgiven him and provided an abundant eternal life with Jesus if he wants to accept it and believe it.

This will be the "last" time that this eternal offer will be made to all of humanity who have not known it before and accepted and believed it to now know it and believe it. However it will be a **continuing offer to believe**, if need be, forever.

The Last Judgement is **NOT** a judgement to hear a court proceeding to determine if the person is worthy or not to be accepted into God's Heaven. No one is!!! It simply is to inform any and all that in Jesus Christ they have been loved, forgiven and accepted into the life of God and now by knowing it they can choose to believe. They can now choose to have "metanoia"—a change of mind and understanding—**REPENTANCE.** This is not a second chance, this will be their first opportunity to believe. This Last Judgement will include the 'approximately' 95 billion plus, or so, humans who have already lived and died on this earth not knowing who they were in Jesus nor the salvation and life He offers.

One last comment on Hebrews 9:27. "As it is appointed unto men once to die, but after this judgment." The Greek word for judgement for sentencing from a legal perspective is 'krima'. However, the word used here in verse 27 is 'krisis or kriseos' from which we get the English word crisis. It means when facing a crisis one must make a decision. So, finally those standing before Jesus in judgement will find out what He did for them and to them they then will have the opportunity to make a decision in this 'krisis'. It is not a second chance at salvation but a continuing opportunity to accept and believe the salvation they already have.

What a great day!!!! What a Good Deal!!! What **GOOD NEWS** this will be for all of humanity to find out at last at this Judgement. Wow!!! God really is **GOOD** after all.

TOPICS TO SEARCH

For those wishing to study further there is ample information in libraries and on the **Web** concerning the history of hell from basically all civilizations and religions going back some 6000 or more years. Satan has always wanted man to view him as important and as powerful as the Almighty God. We owe it to ourselves to arm our self with as much information as to the reality of an eternal fiery hell or as to the non-reality of same.

History of the Devil
Zoroastrian Hell
Chinese Hell
Egyptian Hell
Greek Hell
Druid Hell
Celtic Hell
Plato and Hell
Augustine Hell
Catholic Hell
Dante's Hell
Protestant Hell

Since Adam and Eve man has operated under the concept of reward and punishment. Makes sense to the nature we have. The idea that if one's good outweighed one's evil then this person would attain "heaven" or the happy hunting ground, Nirvana, or whatever you want to call it.

From earliest times to the first recognized world religion, Zoroastrianism, stemming from around 1700 B.C. until the present day the concept of a torturing, punishing, tormenting and everlasting underworld fire would be the fate of the "lost".

With Moses and the Israelites and in Old Testament scriptures this concept did NOT exist. The Hebrew word Sheol simply meant grave and never 'hell'. Even in the New Testament, the three Greek words Hades, Ghenna and Tartaroo, translated hell, never carried the meaning of any type of hell fire. I invite you to take a trip on this journey of discovery!

BIBLIOGRAPHY AND STUDY RESOURCES

Hope Beyond Hell by Gerry Bauchemin, Malista Press, 2007,2010
Love Wins: A book about Heaven, Hell and the Fate of Every Person
Raising Hell, by Julie Ferwerda, Vagabond Group, 2011
Love Wins, by Rob Bell, (HarperOne, 2011)
Word Studies in the New Testament, by Marvin Vincent. Grand
    Rapids, MI: Eerdmans, 1973
"The Gospel of Matthew" Daily Study Bible Series. By William
    Barclay. Philadelphia: Westminister, 1978.
What's So Amazing About Grace. By Philip Yancey. Zondervan, 1997
Hell Under Fire, by Daniel Block. Zondervan, 2004
Mere Christianity, by C.S. Lewis. Simon and Schuster, 1980
The Restitution of All Things, by Andrew Jukes. Concordant
    Publishing Concern, 1867
What Does the Bible Really Say About Hell, by Randy Klassen,
    Pandora, 2001
An Expository Dictionary of Biblical Words. W.E. Vine. Thomas
    Nelson, 1985
On the Incarnation of the Word of God, Athanasius
Church Dogmatics, Karl Barth
The Nature of the Atonement, John McLeod Campbell
The Mystery of Christ and Why We Don't Get It, Robert Farrar Capon
The Mediation of Christ, T.F. Torrance
The Golden Key, George MacDonald
God Is For Us, C. Baxter Kruger

DANCING IN THE DARK, By Graham Buxton
INVITATION TO THEOLOGY, By Michael Jinkins
PARABLE OF THE DANCING GOD, By C. Baxter Kruger
PARTICIPATION IN GOD: A PASTORAL DOCTRINE OF THE TRINITY, By Paul S. Fiddes
THE HUMANITY OF GOD, By Karl Barth
THE MEDIATION OF CHRIST, By Thomas F. Torrance
THE PARABLES OF JUDGEMENT, By Robert F. Capon
THE CHRISTIAN DOCTRINE OF GOD, ONE BEING THREE PERSONS, By Thomas F. Torrance
THE TRINITARIAN FAITH, By Thomas F. Torrance
THE HOLY SPIRIT, By Donald G. Bloesch
GOD IN THREE PERSONS, By Millard Erickson
LIFE IN THE SPIRIT, By Thomas C. Oden
THE GREAT DANCE, By C. Baxter Kruger

ORDER HELL LETTERS

By Paul Kurts

Westbow Press

Order **HELL LETTERS –Exposing the Myth** from the following:

Barnes and Noble
Amazon.com
Books a Million
Ebay books
Christianbook.com
Parable Christian Stores Parable.com
Koorong.com
ANY local Christian book store

Paul is also the author of Trinitarian Letters-Your Adoption and Inclusion in the Life of God, Westbow Press, 2011.

Thank you and God Bless.

Paul

www.hellletters.com